Breed Lover's Guide™

FRENCH BULLDOG

A Practical Guide for the French Bulldog Lover

D1396555

Lisa Ricciotti

French Bulldog

Project Team
Editor: Stephanie Fornino
Copy Editor: Joann Woy
Indexer: Ann W. Truesdale
Design: Patricia Escabi

T.F.H. Publications
President/CEO: Glen S. Axelrod
Executive Vice President: Mark E. Johnson
Publisher: Christopher T. Reggio
Production Manager: Kathy Bontz

T.F.H. Publications, Inc.
One TFH Plaza
Third and Union Avenues
Neptune City, NJ 07753

Printed and bound in China
11 12 13 14 15 16   3 5 7 9 8 6 4 2

Library of Congress Cataloging-in-Publication Data
Ricciotti, Lisa.
  French bulldog / Lisa Ricciotti.
      p. cm.
  Includes bibliographical references and index.
  ISBN 978-0-7938-4176-9 (alk. paper)
  1. French bulldog. I. Title.
  SF429.F8R53 2010
  636.72--dc22
                    2009050715

This book has been published with the intent to provide accurate and authoritative information in regard to the subject matter within. While every precaution has been taken in preparation of this book, the author and publisher expressly disclaim responsibility for any errors, omissions, or adverse effects arising from the use or application of the information contained herein. The techniques and suggestions are used at the reader's discretion and are not to be considered a substitute for veterinary care. If you suspect a medical problem consult your veterinarian.

Note: In the interest of concise writing, "he" is used when referring to puppies and dogs unless the text is specifically referring to females or males. "She" is used when referring to people. However, the information contained herein is equally applicable to both sexes.

The Leader In Responsible Animal Care For Over 50 Years!®
www.tfh.com

Table of Contents

Chapter
1

History of
the French Bulldog

When I first delved into the history of the French Bulldog, I was delighted to find that his past is as unconventional as his eccentric looks. And even a bit risqué. "Ooh la la, you have such a naughty past!" I'd tease my Frenchies as they innocently snored on the couch. I'd discovered that French Bulldogs were prominently featured in slightly scandalous 19th-century French postcards, and while comparing my Frenchies to their brazen predecessors

The French Bulldog's roots go back to the Bulldog, which was created by the British.

posed with lounging lingerie-clad *belles de nuit* (ladies of the night), I'd think how fitting that the early days of this anything-but-dull breed were spiced up with a whiff of notoriety, with some scandals and controversies thrown in for good measure.

The Frenchie in England

To begin at the beginning, here's the first "shocking" revelation from the petit Frenchman's past: The French Bulldog originated in—wait for it—England! Although now a distinct breed in its own right, the French Bulldog's roots go back to the Bulldog (commonly, although incorrectly, called the English or British Bulldog). The traditional larger Bulldog was created by the British, and purists still consider it the only "true" Bulldog. After 1835, however, the breed now synonymous with British character and determination began to change, eventually resulting in several new breeds, including his smaller, less "bully" French cousin.

Blood "Sports"

In 1835, British parliament finally succeeded in banning once-popular blood "sports" including bullbaiting, bearbaiting, and dog-fighting. Suddenly, thousands of Bulldogs bred for those purposes found themselves without a job. The common practice of using Bulldogs as a "natural meat tenderizer" was also

HOW NOT TO GET CAUGHT IN THE WEB

Help! There aren't any Frenchie breeders in my area, so I'm looking online. How can I tell who's reputable from a website? I don't want to buy from a puppy mill, broker, or backyard breeder.

Websites can be very deceptive, says the French Bulldog Rescue Network (FBRN), and folks who want a pet Frenchie but have no background in the breed can be easily tempted by flashy sites and cute puppy pictures. Here's its list of warning signs to watch for when surfing—if two or more red flags pop up immediately or during later discussions—it's buyer beware!

1. Website accepts PayPal or credit cards online.
2. Seller demands a nonrefundable deposit.
3. Website doesn't proudly display photos and pedigrees of their dogs.
4. Seller doesn't health test parents of puppies or compete in official dog shows (conformation events).
5. They can't—or won't—provide references from their veterinarian or former puppy purchasers.
6. There is no written health guarantee (of at least one year) for puppies.
7. Seller doesn't belong to any recognized dog clubs or breed organizations.
8. Seller uses sales pressure tactics, e.g., "This puppy could be gone tomorrow!"
9. Seller is willing to ship "worldwide"—anywhere, anytime.
10. Puppies are always available, and seller offers to provide the exact gender and color you want. Seller also sells many other breeds on website.
11. Seller is offended when asked any of these questions.

outlawed. (Butchers used Bulldogs to attack livestock just before slaughter, causing a final adrenaline rush through the animals that tenderized their flesh.)

The Bulldog Gets Smaller

With their cherished breed's future in jeopardy, some dedicated Bulldog fanciers responded by changing the focus of their breeding programs to produce lovers, not fighters. Their goal was to give the Bulldog a new companion role by developing the more mellow temperament the breed is known for

The French refined the Bulldog's look, aiming for a sweeter expression and a less overdone appearance overall.

today while still preserving his classic "bully" look. Others chose to take the breed in new directions. Some crossbred Bulldogs with terriers to increase their speed and agility, eventually creating a new breed called the Staffordshire Terrier. Still others focused on downsizing the Bulldog into a smaller, lap-sized package, mostly in the 16- to 25-pound (7.5- to 11.5-kg) range.

By the 1850s, these Miniature or Toy Bulldogs were a common sight in the London, Nottingham, and Birmingham areas, and in 1859, a smaller weight division was officially established for these scaled-down Bulldogs. In 1860, some extra-lightweight bullies were even exhibited at dog shows in a special Bantam Bulldog class—for bullies under 12 pounds (5.5 kg)!

British purists deplored the trend toward smaller Bulldogs. How utterly shameful to diminish and degrade England's national symbol by breeding runts, they scolded.

WHAT IS A BREED CLUB?

Simply put, a breed club is an association whose members share a common interest in one particular type of purebred dog. It's where you'll find individuals just as crazy about one breed as you are, whether they're pet owners, breeders, trainers, or interested in competitive activities. These enthusiasts are generally referred to as "fanciers" by those in the dog world (and "obsessive" by those who aren't).

The US national breed club for the French Bulldog is the French Bull Dog Club of America (FBDCA), which can be found at www.frenchbulldogclub.org.

Still, the undersized Bulldog had his own fans. Artisan workers in England's cottage industry gave the small bullies a new career as on-the-job companions, finding their long, often tedious hours of craftwork of sewing, spinning, weaving, and lacemaking passed more pleasantly with a little Bulldog at their feet or on their laps. An added bonus for workers during this less sanitized era: Having a little "bully" nearby meant less bother from ever-present fleas, which preferred a furry body to humans. As well as being flea magnets, these Toy Bulldogs also provided the valuable service of keeping rodent populations down in their artisan homes, which were also their workspaces.

The Frenchie in France

As the little Bulldogs settled into their new, less strenuous occupations, however, many of their owners were ending up unemployed due to the technological advances of the Industrial Revolution. Crafters and artisans were hit hard by the introduction of new machinery that could complete tasks faster than their skilled hands could. Among the many thrown out of work were lacemakers in the Midlands areas of Nottingham, Birmingham, and Sheffield, where the new little Bulldogs were especially prized. They responded by choosing to leave England for new parts of the world where their delicate handwork was still appreciated. Joining them were lacemakers who had embraced the new-fangled machine-powered looms, only to find themselves under attacks from Luddites, a radical group dedicating to smashing new equipment in an effort to force a return to handwork.

The French welcomed the skills of these transplanted Brits, many of whom settled in Normandy—and also welcomed their little Bulldog, admiring his slightly peculiar, comical appearance. Before long, *les petites bouledogues* were attracting attention in other parts of France as well. City dwellers discovered their charms, and the miniature Bulldogs became especially popular with the working class in Paris, where cafe owners, butchers, and cheese merchants valued the wee Bullies as "shop-dog" companions and for their rat-catching abilities.

The Bulldog's French Twist

Soon Parisiennes and other French breeders began reproducing these small Bulldogs themselves—but with their own French twist. While the French loved the little Bulldog's pushed-in faces, they weren't as fond of his other exaggerated features, so typical of England's larger Bulldog: bowed front legs, a pronounced dip or "roach" in their backs, and heavy jowls over a prominent underbite. They began refining his look,

aiming for a sweeter expression than the Bulldog's "sourmug" and a less overdone appearance overall, crossing their small Bulldog émigrés with Pugs, other flat-faced dogs, and miscellaneous French terriers.

As French breeders worked on straighter fronts and less exaggerated toplines and jaws, they also deviated from the British idea of the perfect shape for a Bulldog ear. Although occasionally Bulldogs of this era were still born with upright or "tulip" ears, English breeders were increasingly partial to ears that folded over naturally, called "rose" ears. This preference was so strong that Bulldogs with upright ears were usually removed from breeding programs and sold as pets. Many of the little Bulldogs the lacemakers brought with them to France had those "undesirable" upright ears, and by crossbreeding them with ratiers (terrier breeds with erect ears), the French increased their odds of continuing and accentuating that stand-up

FRENCH BULLDOG RESCUE ORGANIZATIONS

As the French Bulldog's popularity has grown, so too has the number of French Bulldogs in rescues. To adopt or foster a French Bulldog in the United States, please contact:

- The French Bulldog Village: www.frenchbulldogvillage.com
- French Bulldog Rescue Network: www.frenchbulldogrescue.org
- Chicago French Bulldog Rescue: www.frenchieporvous.org

The French Bulldog eventually became a status symbol in Paris, beloved by royalty and high society.

characteristic.

Not that they cared—the French liked the look of upright ears on the little Bulldog since it was less English, and they felt it better matched the breed's comic, clown-like personality. Across the Channel, British breeders were happy to see the French interest in erect ears (although they weren't later on!) because this opened up a new overseas market for their "culls," i.e., Bulldogs the Brits rejected because of small size, erect ears, or both. George Krehl and Richard Harrison, two prominent London dog dealers of the day, became specialists in exporting miniature cast-off Bulldogs to France. Eventually, so many Toy Bulldogs were sent to French buyers that, by 1860, very few remained in England.

Bulldogs of the Night

As the new miniature Bulldogs with a French flair grew more common in Paris, they also won the hearts of another of its working-class citizens—street-walking prostitutes. These *belles de nuit* quickly discovered that not only did the odd-looking dogs make great sidekicks while hanging out on street corners, they were also good for business. Gentlemen would stop to admire the unusual little dogs, and then once the ice was broken, the women could redirect the conversation to their special services and perhaps gain new clients. So many prostitutes adopted little Bullies as their working partners that a new genre of naughty French postcards was born featuring these entrepreneurial women in mildly provocative states of undress, always accompanied by their faithful Frenchie companions.

By this point, the early French Bulldog looked so different from his large British relative that he was commonly referred to as *le Bouledogue Français*, and he was ready to conquer more hearts. Just as haute-couture fashion often takes its inspiration from the streets, the Frenchie took the leap from having friends in low places to becoming all the rage with the high-society set. Upper-crust gents who frequented the pleasure houses of Paris developed a fondness for the "exotic" dogs they saw so often in brothels and boudoirs. And well-to-do women loved to stroll the trendy Avenue des Champs-Élysées with a French Bulldog alongside, flirting with notoriety by using him as a fashion statement about how daring and decadent they could be.

"Dog du Jour"

Soon the French Bulldog was the "dog du jour" in Paris, embraced as the latest status symbol by wealthy Parisiennes and even international royalty. Queen Victoria's son, King Edward VII of England, and Tsar Nicolas II of Russia both imported Frenchies from Paris as pets, not surprising considering both often travelled to the cosmopolitan center—and took side trips to its risqué salons. Dandy Boni de Castellane, the trendsetting French aristocrat famed for

his elegance and fashion sense, owned a Frenchie named Madame Bouboule, often dressing her in coats custom made to match his own.

The French Bulldog's slightly shocking connotations also made him the darling of Left Bank artists and writers in fin de siècle Paris. Impressionist painters Edward Degas and Henri de Toulouse-Lautrec depicted the charismatic gargoyle in ballet, cabaret, and brothel settings, and the controversial, often scandalous French writer Sidonie-Gabrielle Colette owned many herself. Who knows, ex-pat Americans like Ernest Hemingway, Gertrude Stein, and F. Scott Fitzgerald may have admired Frenchies at salon gatherings in Paris!

The Frenchie in America

While the Frenchie was busy stealing the hearts of bohemian artists and high society, he also caught the eye of another group that would play a pivotal role in developing and promoting the breed: *les Americans*. As the fashion and cultural center of the world during the 1880s, Paris was a mecca for international travelers, and many wealthy Americans took prolonged vacations in this stylish destination. Of course, they noticed the fashionable French Bulldog. Soon the most cosmopolitan of these traveling Americans were returning home with the latest French designs and fashions to show off to their socialite friends back home—along with a French Bulldog or two.

The French novelty dog that proved one's continental worldliness soon became America's latest must-have

American breeders clearly preferred erect ears on the French Bulldog, which are still prized today.

producing both rose and tulip ears on *le Bouleogue Français*, Americans clearly preferred the erect ears. During the early 1900s, Americans scoured France and Europe for the finest upright-eared specimens their money could buy, paying outrageous sums of $3,000 to $5,000. Thanks to their diligent efforts to reproduce that prized characteristic in their breeding programs, Americans generally receive credit for the refinement of the French Bulldog's hallmark trait—he is the only breed to sport the distinctive bat ear. By 1907, importation of Frenchies to the United States virtually ceased; Americans now produced some of the world's finest Frenchies without outside help.

status symbol, and a roaring import trade developed to satisfy the new demand. George Phelps, one of the first Americans to "discover" the breed overseas, was the first to import Frenchies to the United States in 1896. From then until 1902, as many as 300 Frenchies a year were imported. (One notable Frenchie export, insured for the then-astronomical sum of $750, went down with the "unsinkable" Titanic.)

But why import when you can breed your own? Americans quickly started breeding the best of the imports, adding their own influence to the Frenchman. While breeders in France were still

Rise to International Fame

The little Bulldog from France was now well on his way to international fame. As well as going for walks with the Rockefellers, Morgans, and other well-heeled Americans, he playfully sat on the royal laps of Queen Victoria's relatives in Luxembourg, Norway, Belgium, Greece, and Denmark, and enjoyed cuddles from the Tsars in Russia. Around the world, people talked about *le Bouledogue Français*, and even the English took note. In 1893, Richard Harrison, the dog dealer who'd formerly exported Toy Bulldogs to France, became the first Englishman to import "French-ified" Bullies back into

TIMELINE

- **1835:** England bans all blood sports. Breeders begin changing the Bulldog from a fighter to a companion, with some producing Miniature or Toy Bulldogs.
- **1840s–1850s:** The Industrial Revolution drives unemployed English lacemakers across the Channel to France, who take their skills—and beloved little Bulldogs—with them.
- **1860s–1880s:** The French embrace the little canine émigré and start breeding their own version called *le Bouledouge Français*. Wealthy American tourists return home accompanied by French Bulldogs.
- **1880:** Formation of the world's first French Bulldog breed in Paris, France.
- **1893:** The Frenchie comes full circle as the British begin importing French Bulldogs—from France.
- **1896:** The first French Bulldogs appear in U.S. show rings, with 19 honorary entries at Westminster.
- **1897:** The founding of the world's first national breed club, the French Bull Dog Club of America (FBDCA).
- **1898:** The world's first French Bulldog breed specialty show is held in New York City at the prestigious Waldorf Astoria hotel.
- **1898:** The French Bulldog gains formal American Kennel Club (AKC) recognition, making the United States the first country in the world to officially recognize the breed.
- **1902:** Formation of the U.K. French Bulldog club. In 1905, England's Kennel Club recognizes the breed as separate from the larger Bulldog but insists on naming it *Le Bouledogue Français*. In 1912, it relents, finally allowing the words "French" and "Bulldog" to be combined as the "French Bulldog."

England from France. The little Bulldog had come full circle.

War of the Rose Ears

Not all were happy to see him back. The well-respected English dog writer C. Jemmett Browne had this to say about the Frenchie's controversial return to England with a new look: "These bat-eared little creatures, which a friend described as a 'cross between a pug and the measles' have become rapidly in favour with the ladies but will never be popular outside the female sex." Browne also posed the question on many Brits' minds: "Should [the French Bulldog] not be given another name to distinguish them from the animal of which they are nothing but a dwarfed and grotesque travesty?"

George Krehl, another English dealer who specialized in bringing French Bulldogs back to the homeland of the larger Bulldog, further stirred things at London's Crystal Palace exhibition in 1893. As a joke, he hung this sign over his six small Bulldogs on display: "French Bulldog of British Origin." Most Brits weren't laughing though, including another writer who harrumphed: "We English have a traditional affection for our own old national dog and object to the nondescript creatures imported from abroad being styled as 'Bulldog'—French or otherwise."

The French retaliated, saying they didn't want their Bulldogs to look anything like the British version, *mon Dieu*! Worried that the English would try to reclaim—and ruin— *le Bouledogue Français*, French breeders banded together to form the first French Bulldog club in 1880, with the first Frenchie officially registered in 1885. This marked a new attitude for the French, ending their formerly haphazard approach to record keeping. The club also began the serious work of creating a breed standard, aiming to write an official description for their French interpretation of the Toy Bulldogs who originally hailed from the other side of the Channel.

The Americans beat them to it, though, thanks to a series of events often described as the War of the Rose Ears. The stage was set in 1896, when French Bulldogs were allowed to exhibit in New York City at Westminster, the country's most prestigious dog show, in an honorary class. Nineteen Frenchies entered, the first shown in America. The following year, Westminster again recognized the French Bulldog's popularity, featuring him on its catalogue and posters, and held a second honorary exhibition. This time 38 were shown under Judge George Raper, a well-known English breeder of Fox Terriers and (British) Bulldogs. To the dismay of American breeders and spectators, Raper consistently awarded ribbons to French Bulldogs with rose ears, favoring the turned-over ears beloved by the Brits while completely ignored the bat-ear preference of the country where he was judging.

The French Bull Dog Club of America (FBDCA)

The Americans reacted swiftly, forming the French Bull Dog Club of America (FBDCA) in 1897 and writing the world's first standard that same year; it was officially accepted in 1898. The standard strongly identified the bat ear as the only correct ears for the French Bulldog. No bat ears? Not a Frenchie.

Plans were underway for the national club's first specialty show, to be held the following year at Westminster, when FBDCA organizers received some most unwelcome news: Caving to pressure from European competitors, Westminster officials unexpectedly created two separate competition divisions for Frenchies. Once class would be judged according to the American club's newly written standard; the second group would be judged by Europe's standard. Many claimed this European standard didn't exist, although the Europeans claimed that it had been recently adopted by France's official canine organization.

With Westminster just three weeks away, the judge declined his assignment. Still, Westminster officials held firm, refusing to change their decision. Outraged, the

Today, the French Bulldog's popularity continues to rise in the United States.

FBDCA decided to hold its specialty on its own site, choosing the luxurious Waldorf Astoria hotel. Holding a dog show in such a glamorous setting was unheard of at the time, and that, coupled with the expected attendance of the who's who of American society, quickly made the upcoming specialty the talk of the town. The event lived up to the public's high expectations and was covered on the society pages of New York papers. Top honors went to Dimboolaa, a brindle dog—with beautiful bat ears. The War of the Rose Ears was over: British-style turned-over ears were soundly defeated, and bat ears triumphed.

Now that the French Bulldog had an official standard and national club, American Frenchie owners and FBDCA members turned their attention to achieving AKC recognition for their beloved breed. Because Frenchie lovers included many prominent businessmen and socialites with significant influence in the dog world, that happened in record time. In 1898, the French Bulldog became an official AKC breed in its Non-Sporting Group.

The Modern-Day Frenchie

The Frenchie's popularity continued to grow, and by 1906, he was the fifth most popular dog in America. After World War I, however, the Frenchman was displaced by the newest "it" dog: the American-bred Boston Terrier. Numbers of French Bulldogs registered annually in America continued to decline, dipping to just 61 in 1959. That rose to 106 AKC registrations in 1960 but a decade later only stood at 107. The Frenchie renaissance to his current highly popular status began in the late 1980s, and the past ten years the breed has seen unprecedented growth. In 2008, an astonishing 6,963 of the once-rare French Bulldog were registered in the United States.

From the bullpens of England to the boudoirs and boulevards of France to the shores of the United States, the French Bulldog has come a long way.

Chapter
2

Characteristics of Your French Bulldog

When you own a French Bulldog, you quickly learn to expect one of two common reactions when others meet your dog: *"He's so c-u-u-u-u-u-u-u-te!"* or *"He's so ugly he's cute."* Cute the Frenchie is indeed—so cute that it's hard to explain what exactly makes him the epitome of cuteness. Let's take a closer look at what makes the Frenchie the most adorable of breeds.

Physical Characteristics

Smaller and cuter than a Bulldog, stockier and less active than a Boston Terrier, and definitely not a Pug (although often mistaken for one), the French Bulldog is a breed apart. He's a small dog but with nothing poufy or froufrou about him!

Many describe the Frenchie as a big dog in a small package—and that's certainly how he views himself. There's something almost outrageously over the top about him—his extra-large head, extra-wide chest, extra-short (but undocked) straight or screwed tail, and extra-big upright (but not cropped) ears. Yet somehow it

Puppy Love

THE PRICE OF A PUPPY

I'm always taken aback by how total strangers will stop me and my Frenchies to bluntly ask the price of a French Bulldog. The conversation usually goes something like: "Hey, those are expensive dogs. Whaddja pay for them?" To which I politely reply, "They're priceless." The real answer is that prices vary by area and the quality of pedigree lines, but Frenchies are not cheap. Raising Frenchies isn't for the faint of heart or for those looking to cut corners on costs. Puppies are usually born by C-section, breeding is often by artificial insemination, litter sizes tend to be small, puppies require intensive hand-rearing for the first two weeks, and mortality rates are higher than in other breeds. These combine to keep prices high. In return for a not-insignificant investment, buyers should expect a healthy, vet-checked puppy with age-appropriate vaccinations from parents who have passed health testing. You should also receive a written contract stating the breeder's responsibilities to the new owners if hereditary or congenital (present at birth) problems occur within a set period (generally one to two years).

Finding a reputable breeder takes time and research, but it's effort that pays off. See the French Bull Dog Club of America's (FBDCA) website for how to start your search: www. frenchbulldogclub.org.

all fits, although this little gargoyle gives new meaning to the usual concepts of symmetry and balance. The French have a term that suits the French Bulldog to a tee: *jolie laide*. Literally translated as "pretty/ugly," the phrase is used to describe something that isn't pretty by conventional standards but nevertheless has a strange beauty and distinct charm all its own.

Sizing Up The Frenchie

How big is a Frenchie? Well, how big is your lap? That's where the French Bulldog will want to be, and ideally he should comfortably fit. Remember, this breed wasn't developed to hunt, track, retrieve, or herd livestock like many others. Instead, the French Bulldog's most important early role was as on-the-job lapdog, and he should be small enough to fulfill this important function.

Most Frenchies fall in the 20- to 26-pound (9- to 12-kg) range, although some are smaller and some larger. Only the American and Canadian French Bulldog standards put an upper limit on his weight, with anything above 28 pounds (12.5 kg) considered as a disqualification for show purposes. The original (now revised) 1897 American standard stated males should be under 22 pounds (10 kg) and females under 20 pounds (9 kg), but 100 plus years later, most are larger. Generally, a Frenchie in good condition

The Frenchie is often described as a big dog in a small package.

will not weigh more than 33 pounds (15 kg) or less than 18 pounds (8 kg). You may be surprised how heavy they are when you pick them up. Solid bone and muscle, the Frenchman weighs more than his small stature suggests.

Coat Type

Part of the Frenchie's appeal is his short, fine, smooth coat. A special bonus is that it's highly pettable! Slightly loose and smooth to the touch, the coat is made for stroking. The French Bulldog will make it obvious that he loves to be petted (in

Some fawn Frenchies have dark faces and are termed "black-masked fawns."

Color Your World

Frenchies come in a wonderful variety of colors and color patterns. Whatever your preference, enjoy the color choices the breed has to offer—but beware of those who breed exclusively for color over health or who charge extra for "rare" colors that are actually disqualifications.

Brindles

First are the beautiful brindles, the breed's basic color. (Brindling is actually a coat pattern, not a color, but we'll leave that distinction to color theorists.) Think of the Frenchie as a fawn dog with a dark overlay so thick that only a few "stripes" or flecks of the fawn base show through. Like a black dress, brindles are elegant, always in fashion, and utterly indispensable. Brindle patterns range from very dark—almost (but never completely) black in appearance, with just a few lighter streaks of color—to very bright "tiger-striped" flashy brindles and everything in between. Many brindles also have white markings on their chests and sometimes on their faces and/or feet.

Fawns

Then come the fawns, with no overlay of brindling at all. Fawns run the color spectrum from tawny tans to rich reds to very pale creamy hues. Some give names to these fawn shades, such as butterscotch, café au lait, honey, or

fact, he may demand it!), and you'll enjoy it too.

The coat requires minimal grooming, but those who expect never to find hairs in their home will be disappointed. Aside from a very few hypoallergenic dogs (who still shed dander), all dogs shed. A Frenchie will not leave a flurry of fur about your house like some long-coated dogs, but he does shed, generally more in the spring and fall. Shedding is easily controlled with grooming (see Chapter 5).

golden cream, but these are subjective descriptions, not true terminology. Some fawns have dark faces as though they're wearing a mask. Hence their name "black-masked fawns," which also come in a range of fawn shades (e.g., black-masked red fawns). Other colors may have masks, but dark faces are more noticeable against the contrast of lighter-colored coats.

Pieds

Actually a short form of "piebald," pieds have white bodies with brindle or fawn patches—and those patches come in different colors too. So, you can have a brindle pied, a fawn pied, a black-masked fawn pied, and so on. Breeders especially cherish "double-hooded pieds," i.e., pieds with symmetrical patches, or "hoods," over both eyes.

Creams

The "creams" (a very dilute shade of fawn) so beloved in America are not accepted overseas, although many suggest that a cream with a true black nose should qualify even under international standards. Although the word "cream" doesn't appear in any French Bulldog standard worldwide, very pale Frenchies rose to popularity in the United States during the 1950s when "Jo-Jo," Ch. Bouquet Nouvelle Ami won 30 Bests in Show. Her granddaughter Ch.

Ralandi Ami Francine later topped that record with 55 Bests in Show.

"Undesirable" Colors

Certain colors and patterns are considered undesirable in the French Bulldog and even grounds for disqualification in the show ring under some kennel club standards. Ticking, or freckle-like markings in the white areas of a pied's coat, is generally considered undesirable on aesthetic grounds, although no standard specifically prohibits it except England's. Blue is universally verboten, including blue brindles, blue pieds, and blue fawns. (Blue is also described as "gray" or "mouse gray.") "Liver," a solid reddish brown, and a black-and-tan color pattern are also universally banned but occur infrequently. Solid black (black without a trace of brindle) is a disqualification in the United States and Canada although tolerated in some countries.

What Makes a Frenchie a Frenchie?

Frenchie breeders and those who

Check It Out

FRENCHIE FAST FACTS

✓ **Height:** 10 to 12 inches (25.5 to 30.5 cm) at the shoulder on average
✓ **Weight:** 20 to 26 pounds (9 to 12 kg) on average
✓ **Coat:** Short-haired with minimal grooming needs

✓ **Colors:** Brindle; a range of fawn shades, some with masks; pieds, i.e., white-and-brindle or white-and-fawn and all white
✓ **Temperament:** Affectionate, clownish, playful, excels as a companion breed
✓ **Energy Level:** Moderate
✓ **Exercise Needs:** Moderate
✓ **Life Expectancy:** 10 to 12 years

show in conformation know the French Bulldog standard inside out. But if your goal is simply to own a happy, healthy companion, there's no need to obsess over the finer points of the standard. Still, your Frenchie should look like a French Bulldog and have the characteristic traits of the breed: bat ears, "froggy" face, naturally short, undocked tail, stocky, muscular body, and other subtler points such as a roach back and a skull that's flat between the ears. Put them together and you have the essence of a French Bulldog.

Bat Ears

Unique in dogdom, this term is used *only* for the French Bulldog's ears. Bat ears are large and upright, with an unusual shape—broad at the base and rounded at the top. They sit high on the head, not too close together but not sticking out to the sides either. English breeders have

a saying about the ideal ear position: "Ten and two will not do!" Think of ear positions like the hands of a clock. The ears shouldn't be at 10:00 and 2:00 but closer to 11:00 and 1:00, almost parallel.

Very few Frenchie ears fail to stand up. Some thick, extra-large ears take longer than others (causing breeders to hold their breaths during the wait); some go up and down while a puppy is teething for an extra comical look. But with very few exceptions, a puppy's ears should be erect by the time he's old enough for his new home.

"Froggy" Face

No, this is not an insult! In fact, many Frenchie fanciers lovingly refer to their breed as "frog dogs." It's the combination of the large eyes, pushed-in nose, and the extra-wide mouth. To really appreciate the froggy resemblance, turn your

Frenchie upside down and look at that face! As an aside, Frenchies also have a habit of lying with their legs stretched out behind, further enhancing the bullfrog comparison.

When you stare at the French Bulldog (and Frenchie owners all spend a lot of time doing that), you'll notice other details. The eyes are large and rounded but shouldn't bulge as much as a Pug's. Ideally, they should be very dark, and the eye rims dark as well. Now look at the shape of the head itself because another unusual Frenchie feature is his skull—rounded at the forehead but flat between the ears. And large of course, with an overall blocky, square-like shape. (This takes time to develop—often more than a year—and won't be obvious in a puppy.) The muzzle is pushed in but not to the extent of a Pekingese or other extremely flat-faced dogs. The nostrils should be large and open, with a clearly defined line between them. A Frenchie should

The Frenchie's bat ears are large and upright, broad at the base and rounded at the top.

have a definite indent, or "stop" above the muzzle, along with a small over-the-nose wrinkle roll. You shouldn't see a pronounced underbite like on the British Bulldog, and the Frenchie's "flews" or lower lips should not hang down as much either.

Roach Back
The dip in the back should be slight, not as extreme as the Bulldog's. The French Bulldog has a unique topline, although not a true roach as defined in canine terminology. Look for a gentle dip back of the shoulder, which then rises slightly over the loins and curves back down. As a result, the French Bulldog's rear legs are *slightly* longer than those of his front.

What Does "The Influence of Sex" Mean?
This section of the French Bulldog standard simply refers to gender differences, meaning that Frenchie characteristics are more prominent in a male than a female. For example, the breed's large head, brawny build, and deep chest are more obvious on males. If that's the adult look you like, you may want to consider a male Frenchie.

Most French Bulldogs will tolerate cats, especially if they were raised with them.

Living With the French Bulldog

Pardon me while I step onto the soapbox for a moment. I strongly believe that a key reason today's shelters are full of cast-off canines is due to a mismatch between the dog's personality and that of the human who selected him. Personally, I think that Frenchies are perfect, but that's because they're right for me and my needs. But do they match yours?

Barking and Snoring

Frenchies don't bark a lot, although there are exceptions—like my own Mitsy! It was a full year before Beau, my first Frenchie, amazed the both of us with a little woof. But they do snore! French Bulldog owners find that adorable, but if you don't, you won't like a Frenchie. Most also have a remarkable repertoire of other unusual sounds—snorts, snuffles, and the famous unearthly Frenchie "death yodel" featured on many YouTube videos.

Companionability

Today, most of us aren't looking for a dog to round up the sheep, retrieve birds, or pull sleds. We want a good companion—and that's the French Bulldog's specialty. He's a champion cuddler and a gifted comedian who never fails to let you know how much he enjoys your company. He'll make you smile when nothing else can. Many remark how human-like he is, with his expressive wrinkly face that shows such a range of emotions, and how in tune he is to his humans' needs. He wants nothing more than to love you and be loved in return.

If a French Bulldog is aggressive toward humans, something's wrong. But thanks to his distant Bulldog fighting heritage, these dogs can have an edge. Generally, the Frenchie doesn't start fights but certainly won't back down if challenged, making early socialization a must.

THE FRENCH BULLDOG'S MANIFESTO

What does my French Bulldog think about all those people who insist that he's a Pug?

Canadian French Bulldog breeder and blogger Carol Gravestock (Absolut Bullmarket) channeled the minds of her Frenchies about 15 years ago, after they'd repeatedly endured misinformed comments on walks through High Park in Toronto, Ontario. Gravestock's translation of her French Bulldogs' outraged sniffs and snorts became an instant classic, an anthem for annoyed Frenchies and their owners everywhere. The text (below) was proudly emblazoned on T-shirts, along with a line drawing of a purple Frenchie by artist/sculptor Becca Williams. The "What Am I?" T-shirt is still available today through the French Bulldog Rescue Network, with proceeds to aid second-chance Frenchies, at www. frenchbulldogrescue.org.

> *I am not a pig. I am not a Pug.*
> *My ears haven't been cropped. My tail hasn't been docked.*
> *I didn't run into a wall or get hit in the face with a frying pan.*
> *I do not bite (but my owner might).*
> *That noise is how I breathe—I am not growling at you or your child.*
> *Most of all … I am NOT "so ugly I'm almost cute"—and anyone who would say that is so stupid they're almost smart.*
> *I am a French Bulldog and I am PERFECT in Every Way!*

With Kids

Frenchies have no problems with the rough-and-tumble play of young ones, as long as the children understand the basic rules of canine–child interaction, such as no pulling of those big ears, no hitting, and no kicking. A Frenchie's tolerance has its limits, and children too young to behave properly around dogs may test his patience. Also, the Frenchie's short, spirited play sessions may be too lively for children under two, who can be easily bowled over by his sturdy body and blocky head. Of course, there are always exceptions to this general rule, and decisions should be made on a case-by-case basis, depending on each Frenchie and each child's individual temperament and upbringing.

With Other Dogs

Some Frenchies insist on being top dog in a multi-dog home; fortunately, many larger dogs are happy to let these little Napoleons boss them around. Surprisingly, girls can be the worst offenders, usually disagreeing most about sharing space with other unspayed females. Neutering helps, but generally it's best to choose a Frenchie of the opposite sex if adding another. Most French Bulldogs will tolerate cats—except mine, who think that they're large squirrels and want to chase them. If they're raised with cats, it's usually not an issue.

Flatulence

Then there's the matter of the famous "French perfume." Some Frenchies pass gas powerful enough to clear a room. Often this can be lessened with the proper food, but some just seem prone to flatulence. You have been warned!

Health Considerations

Mention must also be made of the French Bulldog's special health considerations, including breathing issues, back, hip, and knee problems, and allergies. (These are discussed in depth in Chapter 9.) Generally, the French Bulldog is a sturdy, fairly sound dog with a few special structural problems that require careful choices by breeders. If well bred, Frenchies generally won't have more problems than most other breeds. But if not—or if genes turn out wrong, despite a breeder's best intentions—you may find your vet on speed dial and your credit card maxed.

Environment

The French Bulldog is a highly adaptable dog, comfortable in a variety of settings. He's happy to live in the country but also does very well in city and suburban environments, including apartments and condos with small yard spaces. His moderate activity level and smaller size make him easy to live with; he's not hyper in the house (although a big fan of rowdy play sessions) and is generally satisfied with short- to medium-length walks. If you're occasionally up for more, he'll certainly do his best to accommodate you. Mine are content to lie at my feet for hours while I work at the computer, then eager for action when I ask who's ready for a walk. It's easy to take three with me in my small car on outings, and they all fit comfortably on my couch.

The Frenchie is definitely not the dog for those who want an "outside" or "kennel" dog. *Sacre bleu!* The Frenchie should be in your home, and he'll do his best to stay right at your feet, share your bed, and accompany you everywhere, including the bathroom. Which brings us to the next point: If you're out every night, forget about a Frenchie. The cruelest thing you can do to this breed is ignore him or deprive him of your company. Bred specifically as a companion, he needs—and yes, demands!—attention. So, if you prefer an aloof, less in-your-face dog, please consider another breed.

Exercise Requirements

Frenchies love their lap time and naptime, but they also enjoy getting out and about to see the world. If you're short on time, they're happy to run around in your (fenced) backyard, but ideally they prefer a short 15- to 20-minute walk or two a day. However, the French Bulldog is not for you if you're looking for a long-distance jogging partner. He's more of a sprinter, up for short bursts of energy but quite content to share the couch with you in between. He's also not a swimmer. The rare Frenchie can swim, but most sink like stones due to their chunky front-loaded body and short muzzle. Also, the Frenchie is *extremely* heat sensitive, again due to that flat face, and outdoor activities on hot days require special precautions. In hot climates where you're not comfortable without fans or air-conditioning, he probably won't be either.

Most Frenchies are not swimmers, so supervise them around bodies of water.

Trainability

If you're looking for an absolutely obedient, quick-to-train, do-it-right-every-time-on-command dog, you may want to pass the Frenchie by. Not that they aren't smart! It's more that your relationship with him will be closer to partners than master and servant. (If fact, many Frenchie owners cheerfully admit that they wait on their Frenchies hand and foot.) Be careful, however, not to fall into the oh-so-easy trap of letting your adorable Frenchie get away with whatever he likes, since even his naughty antics can seem cute. He will quickly become the boss of you, with possible aggression problems if you don't set house rules early.

Undoubtedly, the best thing about Frenchies is how much they make you laugh. My life has changed for the better since these comedians entered it. My sister, who has three of my Frenchies, often remarks how hard it is to explain to others just how entertaining these funny dogs are. Send in the clowns? Don't bother—the Frenchie is here!

Chapter 3

Supplies for Your French Bulldog

The Frenchie's needs are simple. Topping his wish list is time with you; what comes after that can be as deluxe or bare bones as you like, after some basic needs are met. Most owners love to treat their little clowns to designer collars and tons of toys, but the Frenchman will be quite content without fancy frills. Here are items to consider for starters—how far you pamper him after that is up to you. But he is the former companion of royalty and Rockefellers after all, so feel free to indulge!

Bed

If your Frenchie shares your bed, make it safe and easier to jump on and off with a slip-free, padded mat below. And if your bed is extra high or your Frenchie is elderly, you may need dog stairs beside

Easy clothing options for Frenchies include sweaters and T-shirts.

your bed to prevent bad landings that could hurt his back.

Wherever he spends his nights, he'll still need a day bed of his own for downtime and naps. In fact, a Frenchie can never have too many beds. And if you don't want him on your favorite chair or couch (good luck with that!), you'll need to provide tempting alternatives.

When shopping for a bed that suits your fashionable Frenchie, and ideally your decor as well, keep practical issues in mind. This dog loves to chew, and his strong jaws are very effective, so anything wicker is out. Few Frenchies can resist gnawing wicker, and if swallowed, sharp pieces can cause serious internal damage. Frenchies also love the challenge of de-stuffing cushiony beds, so do your best to defeat this urge by sticking to tough, thick fabric covers. Minimalism is best.

Clothing

Regardless of whether you're in the clothing-crazy or fur-only camp, your Frenchie may need two very practical coats for his wardrobe: a winter coat in cool climes and a "cool coat" for hot temperatures. (See sidebars "Hot Dogs: Coping with the Heat" and "Cool Stuff" for more on hot- and cold-weather choices.)

Collar

Frenchies are what's called a "head breed" in dog show circles. For judges, that means

PUPPIES AND TOYS

Like babies, puppies need toys for mental stimulation, such as Nylabones, to learn how to play and occupy themselves, and as outlets for chewing while teething. So it's not surprising that many infant toys make good puppy toys because special precautions are taken to eliminate anything that can easily be torn off and swallowed, and safety-approved toys will also be free from harmful chemical, dyes, or lead. Make sure that the toys are large enough that your puppy won't swallow them whole (it happens!) and tough enough to withstand serious chewing.

that the French Bulldog's head deserves special attention when selecting a winner; for the rest of us, it means that his head is one of his most striking features. And nothing sets off that beautiful Frenchie head like a special collar.

To select an appropriately sized collar, be sure that you can easily slip two fingers under the collar when fastened.

Types

Whichever type of collar you choose, never, ever leave your Frenchie alone with a collar on. It may sound far-fetched, but curious Frenchies have managed to catch their collars on the most unlikely objects when home alone. In their panic to get loose, they could begin to hyperventilate, with disastrous results.

Flat Collars

Basic flat collars—as well as far-from-basic variations with silver, rhinestones, and beads—come in two types: buckle and quick-release snap. Most are made of leather or nylon, although you'll also find exotic beaded versions strung over wire for dress-up occasions and eco-friendly choices, such as organic cotton and hemp. It's your choice, depending on your preference and pocketbook. Most are adjustable, but because there's a big difference between puppy- and adult-sized necks, buy what's appropriate for your Frenchie's current needs.

Harnesses

Although your Frenchie has a thick neck, it's more sensitive than it seems. Like his English cousin, many French Bulldogs have small, easily damaged trachea (windpipes) that are prone to tracheal collapse. And some Frenchies are their own worst enemies, pulling hard against their leashes when excited while cheerfully ignoring their diminishing air supply. My solution is a very wide collar, which lessens harm to the throat—and training my dogs to walk nicely.

A popular solution, though, is a harness. These solve the problem of a collar cutting into your Frenchie's neck, but don't expect it to solve the pulling problem! As one old-school trainer told me, when you put a harness on your dog, it simply teaches him to pull more effectively.

If you like harnesses for everyday or occasional use, you're in luck. There are so many fashionable choices, in a variety of styles ranging from strap-like loops to mini-body harnesses, which are often made of mesh and are very comfortable. It's best to take your Frenchie with you when buying because his deep chest needs special fitting. For an online order, include chest

A crate can keep your Frenchie safely confined for short periods when you're not there to supervise him.

(and head!) measurements.

Crate

A quality crate isn't cheap but will serve your Frenchie well his entire life. Consider his adult size and choose a crate large enough for him to comfortably stand, sit, and turn around in once full grown. It's better to err on the side of too much room than too little. This crate will look enormous for your petite pup—and actually is far more room than a puppy should initially have during housetraining. To solve this without buying both a puppy crate and an adult size later, go big but look for crates with a movable divider. This will let you initially reduce the space available, expanding it as housetraining progresses.

Types of Crates

You'll see many crates on the market, but choices basically group into four types: wire, hard-sided plastic, canvas/cloth, and decorator "designer" crates.

Wire Crates

My strong preference is the wire type because it allows air to freely circulate, an important consideration for your flat-faced friend whose breathing is already restricted more so than long-muzzled breeds. Wire crates also allow your Frenchie to see what's going on around him while ensconced in his private sanctuary. He's curious and will appreciate a view. When he needs a complete rest, just throw an old sheet or blanket over three sides for privacy and fewer distractions.

Plastic Crates
Plastic crates can be useful if your Frenchie's a frequent flyer because airlines require hard-sided, enclosed crates. Plastic crates are also easier to carry into a hotel or vet's office.

Canvas/Cloth Crates
A new trend in crates is soft-sided, water-resistant canvas crates. These are very lightweight and fold flat for portability or storage. They may work for your Frenchie and are useful for short periods or outdoors, but their mesh windows and doors easily succumb to repeated scratching.

Decorator Crates
Once your Frenchie is mostly accident-proof in his crate, you may want to treat him to a stylish designer crate that matches your home's furnishings. Some of these are absolutely gorgeous, easily mistaken for a piece of fine furniture.

Padding
Whatever style you pick, you'll also need padding for the bottom of your Frenchie's

HOT DOGS! COPING WITH THE HEAT

Heat is not the Frenchie's friend, and he can go from labored panting to serious respiratory distress in no time flat. Frenchie owners are shade seekers and fan or air-conditioning owners who take precautions and avoid strenuous exercise on hot days. Their arsenal of tools to beat the heat include:

- "cool coats," i.e., special cooling coats or vests made of special fabric that retains moisture and cools through evaporation for up to four hours before it needs to be re-moistened
- spray bottles to wet down your Frenchie, as well as water bottles and portable water dishes (some clever models are both bowl and bottle)
- kiddie wading pool filled with about 6 inches (15 cm) of water for quick, cool soaks
- cooler of ice on long car trips; special cooling mats for Frenchies to lie on; and even mini pop-up tents for instant shade that fold up small enough to fit in a handbag

Ask the Expert

COOL STUFF

Can my French Bulldog enjoy winter?

"Absolutely!" says Canadian veterinarian and long-time Frenchie breeder Dorit Fischler of Belboulecan French Bulldogs. And she has the photos to prove it. Dr. Fischler's website www.belboulecanfrenchbulldogs.ca is filled with happy shots of her cross-country skiing on the Fischlers' 40-acre property near Ottawa, Ontario, trailed by a small herd of romping Frenchies. "As a short-haired breed, every Frenchie needs a good winter coat in cold temperatures," says Dr. Fischler, who recommends fleece-lined coats with weatherproof exteriors and adjustable belly and neck Velcro closures for warmth and easy dressing. Dr. Fischler also advises some type of booties for Frenchies who walk on streets and sidewalks where salt or de-icing chemicals are used. Although she hasn't tried paw wax for her Frenchies' feet on their winter outings, Dr. Fischler feels that it would also work well for protection. Dr. Fischler warns that a Frenchie's upright ears are susceptible to frostbite, and outdoor winter activities should be very short when temperatures drop below 5°F (-15°C) and wind chills are extreme.

crate. Large blankets folded over can do the job, or you'll find crate pads made just for that purpose. Many have extra padding around the edges, like bumper pads for babies' cribs. Remember, your Frenchie will spend hours alone in his crate from time to time, so stay away from crate pads that he can easily tear or chew. And to ensure his safety, always, always remove your Frenchie's collar before crating.

Ex-Pen

Once you use an exercise pen, or "ex-pen," you'll wonder how you managed without. A linked series of wire gates that are unattached at either end, ex-pens fold up flat when not in use. The beauty of an ex-pen is its shape-shifting ability: Stretch it out to block off extra-wide doorways and hallways, or link the ends together to create a free-form enclosed space. While you're cleaning, cooking, or otherwise occupied, an ex-pen can easily contain your dog nearby, so he can still be with you but be safe.

Ex-pens come in various heights, and new puppy owners often buy a fairly low one that they can easily reach over to pick up their puppy. If you want to use the same ex-pen later, it's best to buy at least a 30-inch (1-m) height because Frenchies can jump! Another tip: For outside use, secure the ex-pen with tent pegs, or you might see that ex-pen "going for a walk" with your strong Frenchie inside.

Food and Water Bowls

Think simple for your Frenchie's dishes. Stainless steel bowls for food and water are easy to wash and impossible to break. Thick glass works well too, but whatever you choose, stay away from plastic. Its surface inevitably scratches, harboring germs. Also, we now know that some cheap plastics contain harmful phthalates, which leach into food and water, causing internal damage and allergic reactions. Plastic may also take the black off your Frenchie's pretty nose. Because Frenchies should always have easy access to water, pick up a water bowl for outside play sessions too.

Look for quality over cheap choices, no matter how pretty or cute the design.

Stainless steel food and water bowls are easy to wash and impossible to break.

Inferior glazes will crack, and once that happens, the dish should be discarded.

French Bulldogs love their food, and many of these chowhounds eat very quickly, increasing chances you'll both later suffer from the breed's amazingly aromatic gas-passing. Defense measures, such as using very oversized bowls or adding something like a tennis ball or large stones to eat around, helps slow eager eaters.

Frenchies are small but their heads are large, so select a bigger-sized bowl than you'd first think.

Gate

Like ex-pens, baby gates are also useful for blocking off sections of your home where you don't want your Frenchie wandering unsupervised. Some gates are easy to move from door to door; others require more permanent installation. Be sure that any baby gate you choose meets consumer safety standards. For something sturdier and more attractive, look for metal and/or wooden gates made specifically as indoor dog gates. These tend to be easier to open and close than sometimes-finicky baby gates, and many are so well designed that they blend tastefully with your home instead of giving it a kennel look.

Grooming Supplies

The Frenchie is what show folks call a

"spit-and-polish" breed: He's presented *au naturel* with a minimum of grooming. He doesn't need much maintenance at home either. We'll discuss the grooming supplies you'll need in Chapter 5.

Identification

It can happen to the most careful owner: Your dog finds a hole in the fence you didn't know about, a child or repair person leaves a gate open, your supposedly high-quality leash has a flaw and snaps. Suddenly, your Frenchie is on the loose. Having some form of identification could make a world of difference in getting him back.

Collar Tags

The simplest ID is a collar tag. You can get a rabies tag from the veterinarian, with your vet's office number on it, and also have a city license tag. Both are good backups, but savvy owners also add a tag engraved with their dog's name, address, and phone number. This lets whoever finds your dog call you first (which could save your Frenchie the stress of a trip to the pound). Engraved tags are inexpensive, and many pet supply stores offer engraving services. Because your Frenchie's collar might carry three or more tags, a thoughtful option is to enclose them in special pouch-like containers, or tag totes, to avoid the constant clanking noise bothering his ears.

Tags can rip off, so another good precaution is to have your phone number and dog's name embroidered onto his collar. (Even a waterproof magic marker does the trick.)

Microchipping

Of course, Frenchies can slip out of collars or go on the loose while "naked." Fortunately, technology can solve that problem too. Your dog can carry his ID at all times via a microchip. As small as a grain of rice, a microchip carries unique code readable by special scanners. The chip is injected under your Frenchie's skin between his shoulder blades in a simple, safe procedure similar to getting a shot. No anesthesia is required, and discomfort is minimal and quickly over—then your Frenchie is protected for life. Of course, you'll need to keep your contact info updated with the company that maintains records of microchip numbers.

Leash

When it comes to leashes, I'm an old-fashioned gal. I still love the feel of a beautiful strong leather lead. But why limit yourself to just one when there are so many options?

Types

Leather's my choice for beauty, style, and comfort, but if you have an extra-excitable Frenchie who likes to pull, a leather leash might not be strong enough to curb his enthusiasm. Choose a leather leash that's at least 1/2 inch (1.5 cm) wide for security. Or consider a synthetic option, which you may also need to do if your Frenchie likes to chew on leather. Nylon leashes are strong, washable, last almost forever—and offer enough patterns and colors to satisfy the most serious fashionista. Of course you wouldn't think of putting a metal chain-link leash on your Frenchie. Metal is far too heavy for him (and you) and will encourage the increasingly common misperception that your Frenchie is an aggressive miniature

pit bull, something to beware of in areas with breed-specific bans. Whichever material you choose, check that the clasp is well made and well attached. Frenchies are surprisingly strong and can put quite a strain on a leash.

It's a personal bias, but I don't use retractable leads, mostly because I'm usually walking more than one dog at a time and these "flexi" leads are a recipe for instant doggy macramé. Still, retractable leads do offer many benefits. They expand and contract at the touch of a button, giving your Frenchie the option of exploring up to 16 feet (5 m) away

Choose a leash that's comfortable for both you and your Frenchie.

Check It Out

SUPPLIES CHECKLIST

✓ When choosing French Bulldog supplies, think safety and quality first—then style and fashion second.

✓ Consider the Frenchie's love of chewing and de-stuffing when selecting beds and toys.

✓ Add a crate and ex-pen to your list of more obvious doggy supplies, such as food and water dishes, leashes, and collar.

✓ French Bulldogs need coats for both summer and winter. Other Frenchie clothing fashion statements are optional.

✓ Many Frenchie owners prefer harnesses to collars to protect the breed's surprisingly delicate throat.

✓ Proper identification could make a world of difference in getting your Frenchie home if he's ever lost or stolen.

while still safely on lead. They're also useful for training, especially reinforcing *recalls*. One caution: Save the retractable option until your Frenchie walks with minimal pulling. Flexi-leads let you quickly stop your dog from going farther out, but often this feature is misused. Seeing Frenchies hauled in like fish on a line is not a pretty sight—or good for their throats. Let your dog enjoy a flexi's extra freedom, but only when you're both ready.

Lengths

Leashes generally come in 4- and 6-foot (1- and 2-m) lengths. Unless you plan to compete in obedience, which requires a 6-foot (2-m) lead, the choice is personal. I like a 6-foot (2-m) lead but sometimes use a 4-footer (1-m) for walking my Frenchies in crowds, where I want to keep them close.

Toys

Frenchies just wanna have fun, so let's talk toys! Rule number one for Frenchies: Anything can be a toy, and often the most expensive item you buy will be ignored for something as simple as a plastic milk jug or toilet-paper tube. Frenchies will create their own toys, so it's important to provide safe options—that don't include your favorite household items.

I keep a toy box full of safe toys, handy for my Frenchies to grab when the mood strikes. To keep them interested, occasionally put toys away. When you bring them out again, it's like a brand-new toy!

Have fun finding toys for your Frenchman, but always think safety first and supervise play until you're sure that the item is indestructible.

Stuffed Toys

Frenchies are very aggressive chewers, thanks to their powerful jaws. They also excel at "evisceration," quickly disemboweling stuffed toys, especially if there's a squeaker inside. Although they go through stuffed toys very quickly, it's sometimes worth giving your Frenchie a toy to shred just to watch his enjoyment. (Remember the Frenchie's past—his rat-catching abilities were prized by early owners!) Always remove any parts that can be easily torn off and swallowed, such as eyes on plush toys. Toys for infants are good choices, with stitched-on eyes and other safety features.

Rubber Toys

My Frenchies have never shown much interest in latex rubber toys, but perhaps yours will. It's worth a try, but again take care because most Frenchies can shred and swallow these too. Stay away from any plastic toys containing phthalates because

Supervise play until you're sure that the toy you've chosen is indestructible.

this softening agent is harmful. Hard rubber stands up well, including toys that can be stuffed with food for extra entertainment. (My Frenchies also enjoy trying to get kibble bits out of a large soda bottle.)

Chew Toys

Your Frenchie will love chew toys, so offer him safe options like nylon bones (I have Nylabones scattered all over my house!) and uncooked knuckle or marrow bones. Raw bones will delight him, but are very messy, so spread a large old sheet before you let him have at it. Bones should only be given under your watchful eye, and because Frenchies can be protective of them, if you have more than one you may need to put them in separate areas first.

Taboo Toys

Put these on your taboo list: rawhide chews of any kind and pigs' ears. If you insist on trying them, the first time you're forced to save your Frenchie from choking by fishing them from the depths of his throat will be enough to change your mind. Yes, Frenchies love all of them, but is it worth the risk? Offer a big raw bone instead as a special treat and for keeping the teeth clean.

Chapter
4

Feeding Your
French Bulldog

I believe that canine nutrition is not a religion—it's common sense based on science and practical observation. It's about finding the middle ground between extremes, aiming for a complete and balanced diet. "Complete" means that all essential nutrients are included; "balanced" means that all of those nutrients are available in the proper proportions.

Canine Nutrition 101

So what is a balanced diet for our contemporary canines? Essentially, dogs need six different kinds of nutrients for good health—carbohydrates, fat, minerals, protein, vitamins, and water—in the proper proportions. That's much like humans, but although the dog shares many of our nutritional needs, the amounts he needs are different. Some important differences to note: As much as we love chocolate, it's toxic for canines, and large amounts of grapes and raisins can cause kidney failure in some dogs.

The right amount of fat in the diet promotes healthy skin and fur.

Carbohydrates

Although carbs aren't a natural source of energy for canines, dogs can convert carbohydrates into sugar glucose, which their bodies can use. Sugars, starches, and fiber are all carbohydrates, providing quick energy and body heat, as well as playing a role in protein regulation and the metabolism of fat. Too many carbs are definitely bad, causing diabetes in dogs (a new and sadly growing trend), as well as obesity. Still, low levels of carbs play a role in a balanced diet, and fiber is needed for proper digestion. Dogs certainly don't need as many carbohydrates as humans, but complex carbohydrates from foods such as whole grains, oats, barley, potatoes, and other vegetables have a place on his plate. An abundance of simple carbohydrates from refined grains, wheat, and corn do not.

YOUR PUPPY'S DIET

Growing puppies need more calories than most adult Frenchies, with higher percentages of protein and fat. Some kibbles are already high in both; others will be specifically marked as "Puppy Diets." If your breeder was feeding a good-quality kibble, continue with that brand, making any necessary changes slowly. Start by mixing about 25 percent of new food with 75 percent of his current food, gradually increasing the ratio of new to old. Divide your puppy's total food intake into three meals per day from ten weeks to five months. If he steadily gains weight, you can begin the transition from puppy food to a regular maintenance diet after five months and begin feeding twice daily at the same time.

A good guideline is that no more than one-sixth of a dog's diet should be from carbohydrates, whatever the source.

Fats

Dogs also need fat. They digest it easily and need far more of it than we do. Fat also makes food taste good. (Everything's better with butter, right?) This energy-dense nutrient also contains the essential fatty acids a dog can't produce on his own. Fat helps the body absorb fat-soluble vitamins and promotes healthy skin and fur. Too much fat leads to obesity, and too much in one feeding can cause pancreas problems. Too little means that your dog will turn up his nose at what you offer—and have poor growth and a dry coat. On average, an adult Frenchie's diet should contain about 15 to 18 percent fat. Puppies will need more, while seniors and Frenchies with very sedentary lifestyles will need less.

Protein

All dogs need protein to build and maintain bone, blood tissue, and even the immune system. Proteins are made up of 23 chemical compounds called amino acids—ten of which dogs can't produce sufficiently on their own, so these essential amino acids must come from his food. As a descendant of the wolf, the most natural protein source for a dog is meat, but unlike cats, dogs are able to obtain all of the essential amino acids they need from vegetable protein. This is not ideal, however, because a dog's gastrointestinal system works most efficiently with meat. Generally, one protein source, whether plant or meat, won't provide a balanced diet for dogs. He needs variety. An all-meat diet isn't adequate either; its unbalanced calcium-to-phosphorus ratio can cause serious bone disorders and even heart failure.

Although dogs require lower levels of protein than cats, they need more than humans do. Depending on his life stage and activity level, a dog's protein needs will vary. For example, puppies and senior dogs need more than most adults. Research hasn't set optimum levels yet, though, and opinions vary. Some now think that having 30 percent of a dog's total calories come from protein isn't too much. (Most vets don't recommend very high levels for most Frenchies, however; an average range seems to be 22 to 28 percent.)

However, not all proteins are created equal. Some proteins, like meat and fish, are more easily digested by dogs, while much of the protein in plants may pass through their bodies undigested. So the digestibility of the protein—how much the dog's body can actually use—must also be considered when assessing protein levels. Too little protein causes poor growth, wasting muscles, and a dull coat. Excess protein is usually excreted in a dog's urine, which can be harmful to dogs with existing liver and/or kidney problems.

Vitamins and Minerals

Dogs also need vitamins and minerals. Fat-soluble vitamins A, D, E, and K are stored in the body; the B-complex and C vitamins are water soluble. Unlike humans, a dog's body usually produces adequate levels of vitamin C, although sometimes supplementation is beneficial. Vitamins and minerals do so much, helping with digestion, proper blood clotting, and the normal development of muscle, bone, skin, and hair. They also help a dog's body use fat, carbohydrates, and protein. Don't assume if some is good, more is better, though. Vitamins and minerals must be used in the proper combination and amounts. High levels of some nutrients can interfere with the absorption of others, and too much can be as harmful as too little.

Water

Water is so basic—and so necessary. Aside from its hydrating properties, water plays a vital role in allowing blood to carry vital nutritional matter to the cells, and it removes waste products from your Frenchie's system. Water also helps regulate body temperature, especially important for Frenchies, who are prone to overheating. Your Frenchie should always have unlimited access to clean, fresh water at all times. If your city water has excessive fluoride, chlorine, or lead, consider a filtration system or bottled water.

Commercial Foods

Many dog food manufacturers today are working hard to improve the quality of their products. With care, you can find premium products that come close to offering top nutrition, but many are less than ideal despite their marketing claims of providing "complete and balanced nutrition." The best products may be hard to find but are worth the search, and some are available through online sales. Of course, premium foods cost more, but the payoff is good health and a longer, happier life for your French Bulldog.

When discussing commercial foods, it's hard to generalize about French Bulldogs because what's right for one doesn't always work for another. If there's one thing I've learned about feeding Frenchies, it's that no one food suits all of them! In fact, many French Bulldogs have mild food sensitivities, and some have major food allergies, which means that they need special diets. I find that my French Bulldogs do best on fish-based protein; other breeders prefer to feed chicken. I don't know many Frenchie folk who feed lamb, but some swear by it. Some Frenchies don't tolerate wheat and/or rice, and most do not do well on foods that include corn or soy. If possible, ask your breeder's advice about what foods have worked best for her Frenchies in the past.

Also, remember that variety is the spice of life for your Frenchie as well as for yourself. Even the best premium food will become boring to him if it's all he ever sees in his bowl. Find several that work well and rotate them from time to time. Variety and rotation also help ensure a balance of nutrients and reduce the risk of developing sensitivities to foods fed exclusively. Mealtime's a big event in your Frenchie's day—why not make sure that he enjoys it?

The Dry Facts: Kibble

Dry food, or "kibble," remains the most popular option on the market. It's relatively inexpensive (often due to high grain content), easy to store, and convenient. In fact, I reluctantly feed it myself. I say reluctantly because fresh is best—for taste and optimum nutrition.

I've tried other options but am back at kibble for now. I make myself feel better about that by (a) using the best kibble I can afford and (b) adding "real food" on top of the kibble. Mixing in canned

Kibble remains the most popular food option on the market.

DECIPHERING DOG FOOD LABELS

Carefully scrutinize the ingredients listed on commercial dog food labels. These will be in descending order by weight. Look for kibble with good-quality meat, fish, or eggs listed among the top two or three ingredients. That meat should be real meat, not "meat by-products," a term that covers a range of low-grade protein from nonflesh animal parts, including lungs, spleens, entrails, and so on. The type of meat should be specified—look for a "human-grade" rating for meat protein sources.

Many commercial foods are high in carbohydrates, far higher than a dog's needs, so stay away from labels that list rice or other grains before meat. Grain is often used as a source of cheap filler, so also beware of labels that include many different types of grain or the same grain in different forms. Add up all of those grains—for example, rice, rice bran, rice flour, wheat, wheat flour, corn, cornmeal, etc.—and you'll find that meat is no longer a top ingredient. Look for whole grains, e.g., "brown rice," not "rice flour," and stay away from anything called "middlings" or cereal by-products, i.e., whatever's left over after the grain is milled for human purposes. In general, grains such as oats and barley are preferable to wheat or even rice. Also, stay away from soybeans or soy by-products and corn or cornmeal because most Frenchies do not handle these well.

Cross the dog food off your list if the label lists harmful preservatives such as ethoxyquin (originally developed as a rubber hardener and banned in human food) or BHA and BTA, both increasingly suspect for their possible connection with a long list of diseases. Good-quality commercial food will instead use natural preservatives such as vitamin E (also listed as tocopherols) or vitamin C (ascorbic acid).

Also avoid commercial foods that include artificial colorings, flavorings, or sweeteners. The dyes are added to make the food more attractive to humans serving it, and the artificial flavoring is added to encourage a dog's willingness to eat it.

sardines, mackerel, tuna, or salmon makes the kibble much more appealing to my Frenchies while also providing the omega-3 fatty acids often destroyed in its processing. Other popular toppings include cottage cheese, yogurt, cooked vegetables such as broccoli, carrots, and potatoes, fruits, and whatever else I'm eating that's safe for dogs, including salads. The big favorite is canned tripe. If you can stand the smell, your dogs will love you for adding it in.

Quality Kibble

The long list of kibbles on the market becomes much shorter when subjected to rigorous label scrutiny. From those remaining, owners still need to make decisions about appropriate protein and fat percentages. Think moderation: not too rich and not too high. Lower fat is usually better for a Frenchie (15 to 18 percent) unless you have a growing puppy. As for protein, a Frenchie's needs are mid-range (22 to 28 percent, on average). The latest trend in kibble is "no grains" or even "no carbs," and while many of these are excellent products, they tend to have much higher protein levels, as high as 44 percent. The jury is still out about whether high protein can be harmful, but it's something to watch for. If your Frenchie starts drinking excessively, he needs less protein, and constant scratching could also mean the same thing.

Size

Kibble comes in various sizes. Many Frenchies like the smaller bite-sized kibbles, but if you have an overly eager eater, feed the largest size you can find to slow him down.

Storage

Be careful how you store your kibble. The large-sized bags are definitely more economical but unless carefully sealed, nutritional value deteriorates with exposure to air. I keep a small quantity in a sealed cookie-tin container, refilling often from a large bag stored in the freezer or my unheated garage during the winter. (It's best to avoid plastic containers, which may transfer unwanted chemicals into the food.) Always check the expiration date when buying as well because stores with slow sales may have outdated stock.

Kibble Misperceptions

A common misperception about kibble is that it's better than canned commercial food because its hardness wears tartar off a dog's teeth during chewing. However, dogs chew on the flat of their teeth, not the edges, so any benefit is minimal. One canine dentist puts the maximum advantage of tartar reduction at no higher than 10 percent. And frankly, watch your Frenchie eat—most don't spend much time chewing!

OH, THAT "EAU DE FRENCHIE!"

Why do I sometimes need a gas mask around my French Bulldog, and what can I do about his unique "Frenchie perfume?"

French Bulldogs are prone to gassiness because their digestive tract is more sensitive than those of other breeds, says Dr. Dorit Fischler, a Canadian veterinarian and long-time Frenchie breeder. Dr. Fischler notes that while English Bulldogs are more likely to have full-blown food allergies than their smaller French cousins, food sensitivities are still quite common in French Bulldogs. To reduce the flatulence that goes along with poor digestion and stomach upsets, Dr. Fischler advises moderation: a good-quality diet that's not excessively high in either protein or fat. Choosing a food with a single protein source eases digestion, although finding which protein works best for your Frenchie can take some experimentation. (Dr. Fischler's do well on fish.) Look for highly digestible diets with moderate amounts of fiber, which often carrying labeling such as "For Sensitive Stomachs" or "Limited Ingredients Diets" or "Hypoallergenic." Adding probiotics to food also increases digestibility and decreases gas, although it's best to avoid *Lactobacillus* strains for Frenchies with milk intolerance.

Canned Food

You may not like the smell of canned food—but your Frenchie probably will! It's much more appealing than dry food. Many owners keep a can in the fridge to top off an offering of kibble, hoping that it will help the dry food pass a Frenchie's taste test. Most owners don't feed strictly canned food because it's much more expensive than kibble. Still, it's often a good option for picky eaters and elderly dogs because its high moisture levels help dogs with special medical needs, such as kidney problems.

Quality Canned Food

Good canned food is not that horrid stuff made of mystery meat formed into shapes and covered with gravy. Those are best avoided altogether because of additives and overall poor quality. Look for quality canned food at special pet supply stores—not your supermarket. The search for quality begins, as always, with a careful inspection of the label, looking for whole meats or fish as the first ingredient. Canned food is high in moisture content, and many lower-grade canned foods list water first.

Because canned food is so high in

moisture, the protein percentages listed on the labels seem low compared to dried food. If you're smarter than me, you can do the math to calculate its "dry-matter basis" (DMB), which often reveals that what's listed as 8 percent protein converts to 36 percent protein, when compared ounce for ounce, once the water content is removed, with dry food.

Some canned foods are a mixture of meats, grains, and vegetables, while others are meat only. Avoid those too heavily laden with grains, but if you're feeding canned meats exclusively, it's good to add in some vegetables. Also, be wary of fat levels. Canned foods tend to have higher fat content than kibble (another reason why dogs prefer it!), so if your Frenchie is beginning to look portly, cut back on quantities or find him canned food with lower fat percentages.

Storage
Store all foods away from excessive heat and cold. Canned food lasts a long time, but it does have its limits. When in doubt, throw it out!

Semi-Moist Food
I can't think of a single good reason to feed your Frenchie this type of food. It's high in sugar, promoting tooth decay and obesity. And most contain lower-quality ingredients and far too many preservatives and coloring. It's junk food for dogs. Of course he'll enjoy it, just as we enjoy junk food, even knowing that it's not good for us. Semi-moist food could perhaps be justified as an occasional "treat," but with so many other good-quality treats available that your Frenchie will enjoy, why not offer them instead?

I highly recommend you leave this food at the store. It really doesn't have any place in a balanced diet.

Noncommercial Foods
The benefits of a noncommercial approach are obvious: fresh, quality food with less processing and no preservatives, by-products, or artificial ingredients is more nutritious—and tastes better too! Owners can also individualize meals for their dogs' specific needs.

On the downside, feeding "outside the bag" usually takes longer and can be more expensive. Savvy home feeders find

The scent and taste of canned food are very appealing to dogs.

ways to cut time and costs by sourcing good bulk suppliers, then preparing large batches at a time to freeze into individual-sized meals. Regardless, it's a more serious commitment than opening a can or bag.

Preparing your Frenchie's meals also means taking time to educate yourself about what makes a balanced diet. The quality of most commercial food may be inferior, but those marked as "complete and balanced" must meet standards established by the Association of American Feed Control Officials (AAFCO) for minimal nutrient levels or pass feeding trials to earn an AAFCO-approved rating. Learning proper proportions and ratios isn't outside a typical owner's grasp, but you can't just throw some meat on a plate and have a balanced diet. There are many excellent websites and books to guide you, with such great recipes that you may find your spouse wanting to eat your Frenchie's food. Also, check with your vet to see whether a raw or home-cooked diet is right for your individual dog.

As to raw versus cooked, that's another topic debated with religious fervor. I weigh in on the home-cooked side of the fence, but to make your own choice,

consider the pros and cons discussed in this section.

Raw Food

Meat is the basis of a dog's diet, and many think that it should be served as close to its "natural" state as possible—raw. This philosophy was first popularized by Dr. Ian Billinghurst under the acronym BARF—or Biologically Appropriate Raw Food. Many dogs do very, very well on a BARF diet, and reports of miraculous recovery from allergies are widespread. (My Russian Frenchie with allergies actually got worse, however.) When a raw diet is properly balanced, benefits include healthier skin and coats, reduced "doggy odor," and smaller, firmer stools because more food is actually digested. Raw diets that include unground bones also result in cleaner teeth because the bones are natural "toothbrushes." Obesity is also less of a problem with raw-fed dogs.

Still, those who jump into raw feeding without proper training often don't adequately provide for their dog's nutritional needs, despite their good intentions. Potential problems include an imbalanced calcium-to-phosphorus ratio (meat is high in phosphorus) and low levels of minerals such as copper and iodine, as well as some vitamins, especially fat-soluble B vitamins. Adding the proper amounts of vegetables (which must be shredded or juiced if served raw for proper absorption) can overcome those obstacles. Raw diets are also low in calcium without supplementation from ground bones, bonemeal, or calcium powder. Also, some try to cut costs by feeding game, which can be infested with worms unless frozen before serving, or by using poor-quality, possibly diseased meat.

If you're still willing to take on the BARF challenge, please be aware of two other potentially deadly problems. First, many BARF proponents feed whole raw bones, including chicken necks. There is a very real danger that smaller bones or bone fragments will get stuck in your Frenchie's throat or lodged in his intestines. (Ask any emergency vet about the rising number of incidents due to raw diets.) Grinding the bones and meat yourself can solve this, as does buying frozen pre-ground patties, ready to thaw and serve.

The last problem, though, is the reason why I no longer serve raw. Raw fans pooh-pooh the risk, but uncooked meats expose anyone with a weak or undeveloped immune system to salmonella, particularly infants, the elderly, and anyone with AIDS. You must be vigilant about cleaning and sanitizing all feeding and preparation areas, but there's still the risk of catching it from your Frenchie. Although salmonella won't generally affect adult dogs, it can kill a puppy or older dog. But here's the really important message: Healthy dogs can still carry salmonella, which is transmissible to humans. I learned that lesson after placing a puppy with a family whose infant shared kisses, floor space, and his high chair with his lovable pup. We didn't know it then, but that puppy was carrying salmonella contracted from his raw-fed mother—and the baby ended up in the hospital. I've taken salmonella very seriously ever since.

Home-Cooked Food

All of the benefits of raw with none of the risk is how I view cooking for your dog. Of course, chefs must learn what's needed for a balanced canine diet, and home cooking does take more time than adding a scoop of kibble to the food bowl. Seeing your Frenchie's enjoyment of his meals and his glowing health is enough, however, to make most Frenchie chefs consider this labor of love well worth the effort.

Once you get past the myth that dogs shouldn't eat "people food," cooking for your Frenchie is much like cooking for yourself. Your goal is the same: a healthy, well-balanced diet that combines the proper proportions of vital nutrients.

(Remember, however, that dogs need more protein and fewer carbs than humans.)

Start with some tested recipes, available online or in specific books on canine home cooking, and then adjust for your dog's needs. That's another of the many advantages of home cooking: You can completely individualize your Frenchie's diet while eliminating all preservatives and unhealthy additives.

To reduce preparation time, cook up large batches, then freeze in individual meal-sized portions. Meals can be tasty stews, meat hashes mixed with vegetables, salmon cakes, or even a simple veggie-stuffed omelet. To ensure balance, aim for variety in your home-cooked recipes, and be sure to give a calcium supplement after checking with your vet. Increase or decrease quantities depending on your dog's weight. You're now making all the decisions about what goes into your dog's food, so be sure that you're making informed choices. Do your research, consult your vet, and enjoy learning more about nutrition. You may start eating better yourself!

Free-Feeding Versus Scheduled Feeding

Unless you have a very unusual Frenchie who understands the concept of restraint, I don't recommend leaving food out at all times—also called free-feeding. It will probably disappear in five minutes anyway. I feed my Frenchies twice daily at about the same time, give or take an hour or so. I don't stick to an exact schedule because that would cause anxiety if I'm ever late getting home for dinner or want to sleep in on the weekends. If my dogs are really hungry, they'll let me know by standing and staring at where their food dish should be.

Why do I feed twice a day? I do it partly because eating is so much fun for them that it's fun for me to watch their enjoyment twice. But mostly I do it because a vet I respect told me that Frenchies tend to have sensitive stomachs, and twice-daily feeding keeps bile from building up.

If you have more than one Frenchie, I really don't recommend leaving food down or any special bones lying around, or you may find yourself breaking up fights. Frenchies tend to guard their food, and some are very food aggressive. It's so much easier to feed them on a schedule (and in separate areas, if necessary) than to put food and "bones of contention" away.

Obesity

Don't make the mistake of thinking that Frenchies are "supposed to be fat." Heavy-boned, yes; stocky, definitely—but that's not the same as overweight. Because Frenchies are a muscular breed, they weigh more than most would guess and

Check It Out

FEEDING CHECKLIST

✓ Aim to feed a complete and balanced diet with all essential nutrients in the proper proportions.

✓ Because many French Bulldogs have mild food sensitivities and some have full-blown allergies, remember that no one food works best for all.

✓ Avoid semi-moist commercial foods, which are often high in sugars, additives, and by-products.

✓ Become a fine-print label reader to choose good-quality commercial kibble and canned food over less nutritious or even harmful options.

✓ Noncommercial choices such as raw feeding and home cooking can be excellent, provided you're willing to learn basic canine nutrition to ensure a balanced diet.

✓ Feed a diet appropriate to your Frenchie's life stage. Puppies and seniors have different needs than a normal adult.

✓ For adults, generally look for a highly digestible, single-protein-source diet, with moderate protein (22 to 30 percent for kibble) and moderate fat (15 to 18 percent for kibble).

✓ Feed at regular times, preferably twice a day.

✓ Learn the difference between the breed's typically stocky, heavy-boned appearance and a "full-figured" Frenchie. Avoid the health hazards of obesity.

can look "fat" to those not used to the breed's unique physique. A fit Frenchie should show "tuck up"—his deep chest should taper upward under the loin, and you should be able to easily feel his ribs.

Obesity isn't good for humans, and it's not healthy for your Frenchie either. Aside from putting additional strain on his joints and possibly leading to diabetes, extra pounds (kg) cause your Frenchie's heart to work harder and make breathing more difficult too. I know it's hard to resist with those dark soulful eyes staring at you, begging for another treat, but be

strong! Substitute low-cal treats like mini carrots, broccoli, or even rice cakes if you like to treat him between meals. And, if you're doing a lot of treat rewarding during training, remember to cut back on portions at mealtime. A tip for Frenchies who really like to eat: Add cooked green beans to his meals, giving him more to munch without many calories. Also, make a habit of weighing your Frenchie monthly. When you see him every day, it's easy not to notice gradual increases. Just like us, it's much easier to nip a Frenchie's weight gain in the bud than take off lots later.

Chapter 5

Grooming Your French Bulldog

If the always fashionable Frenchman came with a care label, it would read something like "wash and wear; lie flat for stroking." The French Bulldog comes by his good looks naturally. Not for him the elaborate primping and salon grooming some breeds require to look their best. He combines high style with low maintenance—if only it were so easy for humans! Still, even *au naturel* beauties benefit from a regular grooming regime, and owners should make an ongoing commitment to helping keep their Frenchies chic. Looking his best is good for his ego and also good for his health.

Grooming as a Health Check

Time spent grooming is an opportunity to more closely examine your Frenchie and evaluate his overall health. Is his coat dry and flaky? He may need more fat or protein in his diet. Is he starting to develop a rash on his belly, or are his feet turning red from licking? These could be early signs of allergies or other skin problems in the making. Can you still easily feel his ribs? If not, time to cut back on all those treats! Are any of his teeth chipped, or is tartar building up? Are his eyes clear and his ears free from excessive wax buildup? Is he sensitive when you touch him in certain spots? Does he have any new lumps and bumps? You may notice little things during

grooming time that you'd otherwise miss, so make his beauty time a mini health check too.

Grooming Supplies

The list of grooming supplies your Frenchie needs is short and sweet, just like him.

- antibacterial wipes for face folds
- doggy toothbrush and doggy toothpaste
- ear-cleaning solution
- moisturizing dog shampoo and waterless spray shampoo for touch-ups
- nail clippers and/or a Dremel-type grinding device
- nose moisturizer, such as vitamin E oil, petroleum jelly, or special nose balms
- soft-bristled brush and/or a rubber curry brush
- styptic (blood-clotting) powder or gel in case you cut a nail too short

Other options your Frenchie may need include:

- drinking water additive to help control plaque and tartar (a great complement to toothbrushing)
- fragrance-free zinc oxide cream, a.k.a. diaper-rash cream (for Frenchies whose skin folds need extra attention)
- metal flea comb (depending on where you live)
- special shampoo for Frenchies with skin allergies

Coat and Skin Care

Your Frenchie's short coat is easy to care for but still needs some easy ongoing maintenance. Brushing reduces shedding and helps distribute the natural oils through his coat and skin, keeping his coat healthy and looking its best. And the occasional bath will keep him smelling his best too. Both are easy to do yourself, and your Frenchie will appreciate your "spaw" time together.

Brushing

Most Frenchies love to be brushed, so do it as often as you like—he won't complain! You can brush as little as once a week or even every other week, but if you really want to minimize shedding, up to three times weekly is ideal. Because Frenchies shed more in the spring and fall, increase your brushing schedule then to make things more pleasant for both of you. Brushing removes dead hair, skin flakes, dander, dirt, and miscellaneous debris while distributing scalp oils to give the coat a glossy shine. And don't forget the other important benefits—it feels good, like a gentle massage, and it's important bonding time.

How to Brush

The Frenchie's short coat doesn't require any special brushing techniques or a degree in grooming. Just brush gently and lightly, holding the brush at a slight angle. Brush in the direction the hair grows, which feels best to your Frenchie, but if needed, brush against the grain to remove more fur. Any brush with soft bristles spaced closely together works well, but for extra massaging pleasure, try a rubber curry brush.

Bathing

Your Frenchie will not be as keen about taking a bath—perhaps because most know that they can't swim. They will endure the procedure stoically, however, and it can even be fun. Some lucky Frenchie folk have large raised tubs or

Puppy Love

HEADS AND NAILS AND PUPPY DOG TAILS

All dogs need regular nail trims, and Frenchies often need special attention for their face folds and sometimes their tails too. Your puppy's adorable wrinkles should be regularly cleaned with unscented baby wipes, and Frenchies with very tight screw tails need special cleaning under that area. Regular face washes, nail trims, and tail wipes are all easier to do on a puppy than a resisting adult, so train 'em young!

The Frenchie's short coat doesn't require any special brushing techniques.

dog certainly doesn't need a daily bath or even a weekly one. Let your nose and his coat condition be your guide. I find once every two months is plenty for mine. If you bathe too often, you'll dry out your Frenchie's coat and make him itchy. However, if he has skin problems, bathing him more frequently can help calm the itch.

Use a shampoo formulated for dogs because a dog's skin pH is different from a human's, and shampoos designed for humans are too acidic. For Frenchies with skin problems, look for special shampoos with colloidal oatmeal, aloe vera, or other soothing herbs, and talk to your vet about medicated shampoos with coal-tar sulphur, salicylic acid, selenium, and other options.

How to Bathe

Wet your dog thoroughly, then add water to the shampoo and work it in. Be careful to keep suds out of his eyes. I fold my Frenchies' ears over while rinsing to keep water out. (Some put cotton balls inside.) Work the shampoo into the coat. Rinse well—then rinse again because shampoo residue irritates the skin and dulls the coat. Because my Frenchies often put their front paws on the edge of the tub, I start rinsing at the head and work backward. A handheld shower attachment is excellent for wetting and rinsing, but if you don't have one, look for

sinks and can bathe their Frenchies standing up. But if you're using the tub like me, don't fight 'em—join 'em! I get right in the tub to bathe my Frenchies, singing them silly songs as I scrub. Be sure to use a rubber mat to ensure a secure footing for everyone. Fill the tub with water at about the same temperature you'd use for your own bath but not too deep.

Of course, there's nothing like a bath to remove the accumulation of dirt and whatever else your Frenchie comes into contact with. Bathing also helps keep down "doggy odor." But a well-brushed

Ask the Expert

CRYING OVER TEARSTAINS

I have a pretty cream Frenchie, but the tearstains under his eyes look terrible. Anything I can do to get rid of them?

Start by ruling out any underlying causes, such as rubbing from extra eyelashes or face folds, says Ann Winsor, DVM (a.k.a. "Dr. Annie"), of Inver Grove Heights Animal Hospital in Minnesota, who has many French Bulldog clients. If that's not the problem, try wiping religiously with a contact lens solution containing boric acid (the all-purpose type used in the eyes, to disinfect, and for storage). Its antimicrobial properties sometimes clear up stains, and Malacetic Wet Wipes (available over the counter) may also work for the same reason. If these don't do the trick, the low-grade infection under your Frenchie's eyes causing the stains needs the help of an antibiotic such as Tylan powder (tylosin) (available by prescription or in a few over-the-counter products). Fortunately, this antibiotic isn't one that upsets gut flora. Although dosage is low, long-term use is not recommended. Another antibiotic called tetracycline is sometimes used as well but should never be used with teething puppies. (And yes, staining often worsens during teething.) What about the many home remedies tried, such as buttermilk powder sprinkled on food, Tums tablets, or apple cider vinegar added to drinking water? Dr. Annie says these techniques are all aimed at changing the pH of the tears, to create a less friendly environment for the continued growth of yeast and bacteria under the eyes—and just might work, although she hasn't tried them herself. Tearstains can also be linked to skin problems, so anything that improves the immune system may also reduce staining. Check with your vet to find what works best for your Frenchie.

spray attachments that fit over your bath faucet. Another tip: Put a hair-catcher plastic guard (available in pet supply stores) over the drain to prevent clogging.

Don't let your Frenchie jump out of the tub on his own. Lift him out, wrapped in a towel, and then use another towel to really dry him off well. Keep him inside and warm until completely dry,

which could take a couple of hours. In the winter, I turn the heat up and my Frenchies dry off sitting by the heat vents. Some Frenchies enjoy being blow-dried; mine don't. Blow-drying should always be done by hand, not with an unwatched aimed dryer, because you'll need to constantly monitor your Frenchie for overheating. Post-bath is also a great time

Your Frenchie shouldn't need frequent baths unless he's excessively dirty.

it's a job that has to be done, and it only gets worse if you keep putting it off. Imagine putting weight on extremely long fingernails, and you'll realize how painful curled-under nails can be. Excessively long nails can cripple your Frenchie with every step, throwing off his normal gait and posture and causing splayed feet, lameness, and eventually, permanent damage. Also, as the nails grow longer, so do their sensitive quick (the sensitive inner part of the nail containing blood vessels and tender nerve endings), making them impossible to whittle down without pain and bleeding. Long nails also catch on things like carpet loops and can rip right out of the nail bed. So, for your Frenchie's sake—cut his nails!

I freely admit to being a real wimp about nail cutting. I absolutely cannot stand nicking the quick and drawing blood. That's why I grind my Frenchies' nails with a device called a Dremel. It takes a bit longer, but it's easier on all of us. You can pick up a small cordless MiniMite Dremel at most hardware stores, but if your Frenchie's breeder didn't use one, expect to invest some time getting him used to its noise and dust. This requires lots of treats and patience, but it's worth it!

How often to clip or grind your Frenchie's nails depends on his lifestyle. In the summer, I rarely need to trim nails at all because frequent walks on pavement wear nails down naturally.

for a good brushing, removing lots of dead hair.

I don't usually use conditioner, which isn't needed to control tangles in a Frenchie's short coat. If your Frenchie has an extra-dry coat or extra-sensitive skin, no-rinse conditioners can help, and you may also need to spray it on between baths. For quick fixes after a roll in the mud or when your Frenchie's too sick to bathe, use a no-rinse shampoo.

One last tip, for owners of pieds—using shampoo with a bluing agent gives a whiter, brighter coat.

Nail Care

It's hard to say who hates nail clipping most—Frenchies or their owners. But

Keep an eye on their length and be ready to trim sooner rather than later. Remember, procrastination doesn't make nails shorter—it only makes the job more painful!

Your Frenchie can stand or sit for his nail trim, whichever works for you both. Or you may need a helper to hold him while you clip. For extra-stubborn Frenchies, you may find it worth while to take him to a grooming salon and let someone else do the dirty work.

How to Trim the Nails

Start by simply turning the Dremel on and holding it near your Frenchie without touching his nails. Give him a treat, put the Dremel away, and then repeat the sequence several times a day for a couple of days. Now that your brave Frenchie no longer sees the noise as a threat, start touching his nails with the Dremel—without turning it on. Treat, treat, treat! End your session by turning it on (still without touching his nails) to remind him what it sounds like. Repeat until your Frenchie seems comfortable with having his nails touched and the noise.

Now you're both ready to graduate to the real grind. It's your mission to minimize vibrations from the Dremel and the heat it causes while sculpting the nails. Holding your Frenchie facing away from you in a sitting position on your lap, grasp the nail firmly and support it.

Note: If you don't hold tight, the Dremel will bounce around unpleasantly. I experimented on my own nails first to understand the effect, but you can skip that step. Use the high speed; lower speeds vibrate more and drag out the process. Press to the nail firmly, but keep the Dremel in constant motion as you shape the nail. Holding it on one spot for too long causes heat—and pain.

I find that it's easiest to start with the rear paws because Frenchies don't seem to mind having those done as much, and by the time you do the front paws, they're resigned to the task. Stop to treat as often as you like, but don't quit until you've done every nail (and the dewclaws if your Frenchie still has his). In warm weather, I like to do this outside because the grinding can get dusty. In the house,

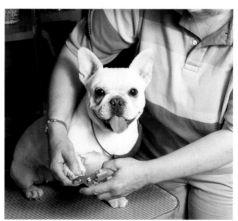
Your Frenchie can stand or sit for his nail trim—whichever works for you.

GROOMING CHECKLIST

✓ This is a "wash-and-wear," easy-to-groom breed.

✓ Use grooming time as a mini health check. Set a regular night to weekly inspect your Frenchie head to toe.

✓ Frenchies are average shedders, thanks to their short-haired coat.

✓ Brush weekly. Every second day really minimizes shedding.

✓ Bathe only as needed, using a dog shampoo. Don't overbathe; once a month is usually often enough.

✓ Keep nails well trimmed. Don't let quicks grow long, or trimming will be painful. Inspect weekly; adjust depending on your Frenchie's needs.

✓ Check ears weekly, cleaning as needed.

✓ Check face folds, wrinkles, and under-eye areas daily, cleaning with antibacterial "baby wipes" if needed.

✓ Put petroleum jelly or vitamin E oil on the nose to keep it moist.

✓ Brush teeth daily with special dog toothbrush and toothpaste. Plaque buildup can also be reduced with drinking water additives and (supervised) gnawing sessions on large, uncooked meaty bones.

✓ Tearstaining can be a problem on light-colored Frenchies, and may worsen when a puppy is teething.

✓ Introduce your puppy to a grooming routine early so that beauty time will be a pleasure, not a battle.

I blow on the nails to keep the dust away from my Frenchie's face.

If you'd rather clip than grind, start by choosing a clipper that's up to the task. It should be large enough and sharp enough to cut through the nail quickly. Too small or too dull will simply smash the nail—ouch! Clippers come as either guillotine-type or special nail-cutting scissors for dogs. I find it easier to see what I'm doing with the scissors type.

The key to success is learning to recognize where the quick starts. It's pinkish and is much easier to see on light-colored nails and almost impossible to see on black nails. It's better to take little nibbles instead of one big chunk, working your way cautiously closer to the quick. It's safe to cut where the nail is thin and pointed; that area is the nerveless, hard core.

Even with the best of intentions, you'll

eventually slip and cut too closely, drawing blood. Don't despair—your Frenchie will forgive you. Grab the styptic powder (which you've carefully placed nearby in advance) to clot the blood, and give extra treats while trying not to feel too guilty. Or press a tissue against the nail (which takes longer for the blood to clot), or dip it in corn flour, which stings less than the styptic powder.

Don't forget to trim the dewclaws too!

Ear Care

The Frenchie bat ear—his crowning glory. Those gorgeous ears need care, but because they are upright, they are open to the air and so less susceptible to infection than droopy ears, which trap moisture and bacteria inside. Some Frenchies, however, are prone to ear infections due to excessive yeast and wax buildup caused by an immune deficiency.

A normal bat ear needs little cleaning; once a month with ear drops should be plenty. But let your eyes (and your nose!) be your guide. If the inner ear is dirty, a simple wash with a baby wipe does the trick. If you see wax in the canal, it's definitely time for ear-cleansing drops, and it's good to make a habit of cleaning them monthly. If the ears are smelly, trouble could be brewing; if your Frenchie starts shaking or tilting his head, trouble's already arrived. It could be an infection, too much wax, ear mites, or even a piece of debris like a bit of plant matter. Whenever your Frenchie holds his head oddly or if his ears are obviously red, inflamed, or have discharge, head to the vet as soon as possible. Ear infections are far easier to treat in the early stages and can become very serious very quickly. You wouldn't want your Frenchie to lose his hearing because you took a wait-and-see approach to his care.

How to Care for the Ears

Ear cleaning at home is quick and easy. Hold the end of the bottle of solution to the base of his ear (but not inside it!), then simply squeeze a few drops inside. Fold his ear over with one hand and gently massage the ear canal at the base of the ear with the other for about 15 seconds. Then stand back! Let your Frenchie give his head a good shake—and be prepared to see some gross stuff come out. Wipe off the gunk with a cotton ball—but don't try dipping inside with a cotton swab.

You know the rule about never putting anything smaller than your elbow in your ear? The same goes for your Frenchie. You can do more harm than good by poking around in there, either packing wax inside deeper or hurting the ear itself. If several repetitions of drops don't seem to help, your Frenchie may need a more intensive cleaning—and that's a job for your vet.

Unless your vet advises it for your particular French Bulldog, there's no need to shave hairs from his inner ear. *Au naturel* is best!

Eye Care

Unless your Frenchie is elderly or has a dry-eye condition, his eyes need little special care. Older eyes and dry eyes appreciate lubricating eye drops, and depending on how serious your Frenchie's need is, you can use artificial tear liquids sold for humans (gels last longer) or your vet will prescribe special drops.

On the other hand, your Frenchies eyes may tear excessively, causing tearstains. While unsightly, staining doesn't usually bother your Frenchie. See the sidebar "Crying Over Tearstains" for some advice, and if these tips don't help, see your vet to check for underlying causes like blocked tear ducts.

How to Care for the Eyes

The French Bulldog's large, soulful eyes do protrude slightly, and because he has a flat face, he's more likely to run into things or scratch them on bushes or even tall grass. If your Frenchie is pawing at his eyes or has discharge, see your vet as soon as possible. If you see a bluish circle or tint in any area of his eye, head to the vet immediately—this means that he's probably scratched his cornea. Without fast attention, this can ulcerate. The fix after that may be surgery and a long convalescence, or if really extreme, the eye will have to be removed. Take any eye problems seriously—better to be a worrywart than to have a blind Frenchie!

Like most of us, your Frenchie will often wake up with a bit of normal "sleep" discharge in his eyes. Just wipe it away gently with a soft, damp cloth. Some Frenchies are prone to tearstaining under their eyes, which isn't as easy to fix. For tips, see sidebar "Ask the Expert." A nightly and early-morning ritual of applying a zinc oxide cream or petroleum jelly under the eyes can help reduce staining as well.

Wrinkle Care

Your Frenchie's wrinkly face is an attention getter, but those expressive wrinkles also need special attention. As a puppy, he will probably just need a weekly face wash, but as he matures, his wrinkles will deepen and can harbor dirt and bacteria. You may find that you now need to clean his wrinkles daily. The easiest way is to keep a container of unscented baby wipes on hand and gently clean his wrinkles at bedtime, taking care not to go too close to his eyes. If your Frenchie's wrinkles smell yeasty or become irritated, he may have an underlying skin problem, such as an allergy. See your vet for advice if his wrinkles become aggravated. It's best not to put petroleum jelly on his wrinkles because this traps moisture and can increase bacteria, instead of making things better. Keeping them clean and dry works best.

Dental Care

Why bother with dental care, you ask? Aside from sweeter breath (which you'll appreciate from this Frenchie kisser), dental care to prevent plaque, gum disease, and tooth loss also means less bacteria in your dog's mouth. Bacteria from poorly cared for teeth enters the bloodstream and can cause kidney and heart infections. So even if you don't care about keeping his teeth pearly white, do it for his health. Vets advise brushing a dog's teeth once daily or a few times weekly at minimum.

How to Care for the Teeth

Here's how to get your Frenchie used to toothbrushing. First, only use toothpaste specially formulated for dogs because there's a good chance he'll swallow it, and dog toothpaste is made to be digestible and taste good too. Some people use a doggy toothbrush; others use a canine rubber finger brush, like a thimble that fits over a finger.

To start, though, simply put some toothpaste on your finger and rub it on your dog's teeth. He'll undoubtedly lick it off, but after a few sessions you'll be able to rub the paste in. After he's used to having his teeth rubbed, move up to using the toothbrush or finger brush. Brush with an up-and-down motion, just as you do in your own mouth. Of course, lots of praise followed by treats helps with this dental training.

There's also a new option on the market: a specially formulated liquid that's added to drinking water. These solutions contain natural enzymes that slow the buildup of plaque and tartar; several brands are available. I find that they work very well. (Avoid any with xylitol added as a sweetener—it can be deadly for some dogs!) However, drinking water additives should be used as a complement to brushing, not as a replacement. Special dog chews and toys, such as Nylabones, and a good gnaw on raw bones also help— but nothing replaces regular brushing.

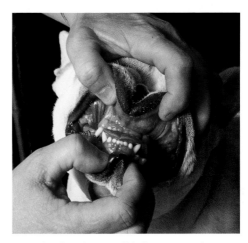

Regular dental care will help prevent plaque, gum disease, and tooth loss.

Chapter
6

Training Your French Bulldog

Many Frenchie folks have a *laissez-faire* approach to training their bat-eared beauties. When their Frenchie refuses to sit or down on command, they'll shrug and say something like "If I'd wanted an obedient dog, I would've got a Sheltie (or Poodle or some other 'smart' breed)." That's partly true. If you're looking for a dog who's eager to please his human no matter what, who lives to train, and who loves repeating exercises endlessly, it would be best to choose another breed. But never make the mistake of thinking the Frenchman isn't smart. Although not eager to follow orders blindly, the Frenchman's very happy to learn if it's fun. He is the philosopher clown, after all!

Why Training Is Important

Dogs share our lives and need to learn manners, the social lubricant that makes it easier to get along, whether interacting with humans or other dogs. As his human, it's up to you to show him what's acceptable and what's not. That's part of the serious commitment you took on with ownership—and failure to teach him the rules of the house and how to be a good citizen could cost him his life.

Sound overly dramatic? Every day, dogs end up in shelters for nothing more than an owner's failure to teach proper housetraining or establish boundaries that prevent canine aggression. It's so easy to simply smile and think how adorable your Frenchie is, even when he's bad, but remember his bull-fighting ancestry. This cute little dog can be very tough and stubborn, and without proper training, can become aggressive. What you think is cute in a puppy can also become unbearable in an adult dog. In a society that's becoming increasingly intolerant of

The Frenchie can be eager to learn if you make training positive and fun.

START TRAINING EARLY

There's no reason to delay training your puppy. His young mind is a sponge, ready to soak in new information. Start working with him at home on your own, in short, frequent, and happy sessions. It's also good to enroll your Frenchie in "puppy kindergarten" two weeks after his last set of shots. Look for special puppy classes, where training is geared for fun, socialization, and a puppy's short attention span, without the possible intimidation of older dogs.

dogs who bite or even nip, and that labels any stocky, muscular dog as a "pit bull," your Frenchie's future could well depend on his good behavior.

Staring at his sweet face, it's hard to believe, but although some Frenchies are very laid-back, others can be borderline frenetic. Some are easygoing, and some are very strong willed. No matter where your Frenchman falls on that range, he deserves basic training. Besides, it can be fun! And nothing's more rewarding than the bond you'll develop by working with your dog.

Think Positive Training

The bad old days of "alpha rolls," jerking corrections, harsh commands, and use of force have been replaced by positive methods. Rewarding your dog for getting it right instead of punishing him for doing something wrong is a much more pleasant approach for owners, as well as for their dogs. A positive approach is especially important for this breed because French Bulldogs do not respond well to training that relies on dominance and submission. In the past, stubbornness was his strength. His ancestors were trained to stand up to bulls without letting go; he's not about to give in just because a human says so! Try to push him around, and he'll push right back. If positive is the way to go for most dogs, it's the only approach for a Frenchie.

It's far better to appeal to the clown in him than to his bull-headed side. A sense of humor is essential. Be patient while he figures out what you want, reward him copiously with praise and treats when he gets it right, and gently show him again when he doesn't. As one of my trainers says, nobody wants to work without getting paid. So give your Frenchie his "paycheck"—reward him with a treat!

Many trainers today use clicker training, using the "click" sound made by pressing a small handheld device, followed by a treat, to mark correct behavior. It's a good technique to learn, although I find it easier to simply reinforce with an enthusiastic "Yes!" and a treat. Using your voice means one less thing in your hands, which will already be holding a leash and grabbing treats. Besides, you won't always have a clicker on you. Find a good trainer (see sidebar "Finding a Trainer") and see what works for you.

Socialization

It's easy to forget, but dog are not hardwired to interact socially with humans. Twelve thousand years of domestication have proven it's possible, but just as children need to learn how to behave appropriately in social situations, puppies must learn how to get along with humans and the world around them. That process is called socialization, and if your puppy doesn't receive proper socialization training at critical stages of his development, it's possible he'll never gain it later—and he'll live a sad, antisocial life.

How to Socialize

A puppy's early socialization actually starts before he goes to his forever home. His mother, littermates, and any other dogs where he was raised all do their part to teach him what's socially acceptable when dogs interact with dogs. That's why it's so important that a puppy isn't taken from his mother too early—he first needs to learn how to be a dog.

Once you bring a puppy home, you take over the next important task: teaching him how to be a dog who lives comfortably with humans as well as dogs. Because the puppy's first key socialization period happens between 7 and 12 weeks, and many Frenchies are not placed until 10 weeks or older, a good breeder will have already started this process. As his new owner, you will then continue socializing your puppy, expanding his world by exposing him to new sights, sounds, people, and events. A puppy learns at this time like no other; what he's exposed to makes an impression for life, so it's important that any new experiences are positive. It's a big responsibility, especially because puppies also go through a second fear imprint period from 6 to 14 weeks, during this socialization period.

You want to take your puppy everywhere, but is it safe? New vaccination protocols mean that puppies will not receive their final set of puppy shots until 16 weeks or later, and their booster shots until they are 1 year old. It's a dilemma! You can't take him to

It's important for your Frenchie to socialize with other places, people, and other dogs.

dog parks, and even a walk down the street could be dangerous when he's not fully vaccinated. (One of my friends' puppies recently contracted parvo from a single walk in a very high-traffic city neighborhood.) The solution is to be smart, choose your locations wisely—and get a puppy carrier. Carrying your Frenchie in a puppy pouch or backpack lets him see, hear, and smell the big world out there without the threat of catching bugs. Of course, everyone who sees your puppy will want to pat him—and you want them to—so carry hand sanitizer and ask people to "wash" their hands first. It's important for your Frenchie to socialize with other people and dogs in a variety of settings.

The more people your Frenchie meets before his first birthday, the better! If you don't have children, invite some over. If you rarely have people over, take him out in crowds and gatherings. Your puppy needs to meet babies, the elderly, people wearing hats and sunglasses, men with beards, people with loud voices—the whole gamut of humanity. Because many puppies are raised by women, it's especially important to introduce them to lots of men. You'll also need to introduce your Frenchie to your vacuum cleaner, the dishwasher, and other noisy things

THE SPOILED FRENCHIE

My Frenchie's so cute, and I enjoy spoiling him. Usually that's no problem because he's laid-back, sweet, and lovable. But is it possible to spoil him rotten?

Oh, yes, indeed it is, says Mary Phelps, Autumn Run French Bulldogs, a long-time breeder and trainer in Minnesota. Phelps formerly competed with her Frenchies in obedience, but today she competes in agility. "Frenchies come across as sweet, demure little dogs," Phelps notes. "But you don't do them any favors by giving them everything they want. Someone needs to be in charge, and if you're not the leader, your Frenchie will take control." Phelps points out that you may not have issues in your home because you're happy to indulge your Frenchie's every whim, but you'll run into problems in public situations where other humans or dogs don't do the same. Phelps uses positive reinforcement, including clicker training, but emphasizes that, regardless of his charm, the Frenchman needs proper training like any other breed.

in your house, as well as traffic sounds, sirens, and airplanes flying overhead. Just don't do it all at once and overwhelm him. (Remember the fear period he's going through too.) Keep lots of treats with you to reward him for bravely encountering something new, but don't coddle him when he's fearful. Just let him have a break and then try again, with more praise.

Crate Training

Your Frenchie should learn how to use—and hopefully enjoy—a crate, but crating should never be a lifestyle for this gregarious, company-loving extrovert. Consider his early history—long hours snoring contentedly on a lacemaker's lap. Does that sound like a dog who'd be happy spending a lot of time alone, confined to a small space? This socialite needs human interaction, so don't overuse the crate, no matter how convenient it may seem.

Teaching your Frenchie to use a crate as a puppy is a valuable tool for housetraining (see section "Housetraining") and also provides a temporary sanctuary where he can be safe while not in your sight. Yes, even the most fanatic Frenchie owner needs a break from constant puppy monitoring, and so do your prized possessions until he's learned not to chew everything in sight.

How to Crate Train

Hopefully, your breeder has already begun crate training so that you can build on it, but if not, it's never too late. Start by making the crate a fun place to be. That means never use the crate as a place to be banished to for punishment. Let your Frenchie play with a favorite toy inside his crate with you still there and the door open. Give him treats to eat while inside. Gradually increase the amount of time he is inside and then start closing the door for short periods—very short, just a couple of minutes. Gradually increase the time he's alone. He may whimper a bit at the start, but don't open that door at the first squeak, or he'll quickly learn that you'll let him out if he cries. Increase your chances of success by putting your Frenchie in the crate when he's already tired and ready for sleep. To keep him from boredom, give him a rubber toy stuffed with frozen broth to slowly lick, or give him a safe bone to chew, like a Nylabone. Some Frenchies also enjoy listening to music or the television while crated.

If, despite all your patience and praise, your Frenchie insists in his typically straightforward Frenchie way that he hates being crated, maybe it's not for him. Try a comfy bed in an ex-pen if you still need to contain him while a he's puppy for his safety. Or dispense with it altogether and give him a special quiet place of his own outside the crate. I have two very large wire crates in my house (big enough for my English Bulldog), and often three Frenchies will curl up together inside. But the door's always open, and it's their choice. I can't remember the last time I closed that door now that my Frenchies are grown and have good house manners. Crating is a good tool, but it's always optional. There's no rule that says a Frenchie must spend a specific amount of time per day in a crate. It's certainly has its place while teaching your puppy housetraining and ensuring that he's safe while you're away, but ideally no dog should be crated for longer

If your Frenchie hates to be crated, try placing a comfortable bed in an ex-pen if he needs to be contained.

than five or six hours, no matter what age. Working owners who can't make it home at lunchtime to give their pups a break should enlist the help of obliging neighbors or consider putting their pup in doggy day several times a week. Once your Frenchie is an adult, it shouldn't be necessary to crate him all day while you're at work.

Housetraining
Now for the really fun stuff—

When housetraining your puppy, try to take him out on a regular schedule.

housetraining! I hear from other breeders and owners that Frenchies are hard to housetrain. I don't know if that's true; the only other breeds I've housetrained were one Boston Terrier and one English Bulldog. But I'm throwing that fact out there because Frenchies can be stubborn, and it may make you feel better to know that others have had difficulties before you.

It also helps if you start with reasonable expectations. An eight- or even ten-week-old puppy is too young to have enough bladder control to make it through the night. Expect to spend a couple of weeks getting up with your puppy in the night to take him out (yes, you should go with him!) or expect overnight "accidents." It may seem like forever, but eventually he'll start sleeping through the night without needing a bathroom break, and you will finally get a good night's sleep too.

How to Housetrain
There are five golden rules of housetraining: Stick to a schedule, never punish the puppy after the fact, learn to recognize and respond to his signals quickly, praise him profusely—and never let him out of your sight!

1. **A schedule can save your sanity.** What goes in must come out, and it does so at predictable frequencies. As soon as your puppy wakes up—in the morning

or after a nap—take him outside immediately. Soon after he finishes eating, take him outside. If he doesn't do anything, wait 15 minutes and try again. Still nothing? Wait another 15 minutes and try again.

You can make matters easier by feeding your puppy at regular times. This gets him accustomed to putting his bodily functions on a set schedule too. It also helps to put him to bed at the same time for the same reason. Although puppies should always have water, withholding water for several hours before bedtime improves his chances of overnight success.

2. **Never punish after the fact.** In fact, let's reword that to never punish your puppy for accidents, period! If you catch him in the act, you can voice a loud "NO!" and then simply scoop him up and take him outside to finish. But there's no point in screaming when you find a new mess or taking him over to show him and scold him. And never, never rub his nose in his messes or hit him with a rolled-up newspaper. Your puppy won't make the connection between the mess and the fact that he made a mistake. All he'll learn is that humans fly into rages unpredictably, for reasons he doesn't understand.

3. **Learn to recognize and respond to his signal quickly.** Watch for warning signs like sniffing, circling, pacing, looking for a spot, and the telltale squat. All are early warning signals that an accident is about to happen. Set your puppy up for success by learning these signals and reacting quickly. When you see any of the above, call his name loudly, run over to him, pick him up, and carry him outside to safety.

4. **Praise profusely.** "Holding it" is hard work, so reward the effort. Take treats outside with you, and reward your Frenchie on the spot. Don't just stand in the doorway and watch. Go with him to be sure that something's happened and to praise immediately. Praise any efforts to succeed as well. If your puppy is heading for the door but doesn't make it, still tell him he's a good puppy. Let him know that you

noticed, and maybe he'll make it next time.

5. **Never let him out of your sight.** Easier said than done, right? Since you can't put your life on hold, use some safety nets. Tie him to your waist while your attention's elsewhere, and be ready to act if necessary. And use the crate to give yourself a break. But as soon as you take him out of the crate—it's outside for both of you!

Other Tricks and Tips

Try taking your puppy to the same place outside so that he knows that you're out there for a reason, not to play. Use the same words to remind him what's expected (e.g., "Go potty.") Crate him overnight, but make sure that the space isn't too large. If it is, he'll use one end of the crate for soiling and save the other for sleeping. Start training right away; don't wait until he's older. You may have to take him outside every two hours initially, but he's learning not to go in the house. Clean up messes thoroughly with an enzymatic cleanser to completely eliminate the scent—and preferably not while he's watching, or he'll think that you're his maid. Limit his space, using an ex-pen or a crate when he's not right in your sight, expanding it gradually as he gains more control. If you're bewildered by a seeming

Treats and praise are great motivators when training your Frenchie.

lack of progress, start charting out events on a paper taped to your fridge. Write down when you feed the puppy, when he goes outside, when he eliminates outside, and when he has accidents in the house. Look for patterns and problem areas, make adjustments, and persevere. If you're doing everything right and still not making progress, book an appointment with your vet. Your Frenchie may have a urinary infection or some other underlying problem.

How Long Can He Wait?

A general guideline is that a puppy can wait one hour for every month of his age. In other words, a puppy who's two months old needs a bathroom break every two hours, a four-month-old can wait four hours, etc., until he reaches six months or so. After that, most puppies can wait accident-free until you return home from work, and they'll sleep through the night without needing to relieve themselves. Adjust your schedule accordingly by coming home at lunch if you're working or by having a friendly, reliable neighbor take him out.

Basic Obedience Training

Whether you're training a puppy or an adult, approach your training sessions with a big dollop of humor. It's not life or death if your dog doesn't understand right away, and mistakes are allowed. Keep your voice upbeat and enthusiastic. If you don't think it's enjoyable, your Frenchie certainly won't.

Communication

If something's not getting through, stop a moment to look at what you're doing and saying from a canine perspective. Think like a dog to try to understand why your Frenchie isn't getting your message. Is your body language confusing? Perhaps you're saying one thing while your posture and actions say another. Are you rewarding him at the right moment so that he makes the connection when he's responded correctly?

Treats

Because training your Frenchie will take a lot of treats, use something you can easily break into tiny pieces. (A large size isn't important; how often he gets the treat is!) I like to use something soft that breaks up easily, like sausage-shaped meat rolls that

Check It Out

TRAINING CHECKLIST

✓ Frenchies are smart but can be stubborn and not as eager to please as some breeds.

✓ Being cute doesn't give your French Bulldog a free pass to excuse bad behavior. He still needs and deserves proper training to understand limits and house rules.

✓ A positive approach to training is a must, along with a sense of humor.

✓ Be consistent and patient. Emphasize fun, treats, and rewards. Make him think what you want him to do is really his idea.

you can cut into very small pieces. Bits of cheese or string cheese also work or fragments of dried liver. (Too many liver treats gives most Frenchies the runs, so although they love it, use liver cautiously.) Some people even use toasted oat cereal. Treats should be small and soft enough so that your Frenchie will scarf them down quickly; you don't want to spend your training time waiting for him to chew and swallow. Reduce his meal proportions if needed to compensate for his treat intake.

As your Frenchie begins to understand what you're asking, you can start to expect more from him, withholding treats for half-hearted efforts or gently indicating he's wrong with words like "oops! " or "try again." (Try to refrain from a harsh "NO!" or the stubborn Frenchman will stop listening.) Lavishly reinforce the positive and don't reward the negative. Not right? No treat. He'll get the point quickly! If treats don't work, your task is more difficult. You'll have to find what does motivate him, be it a favorite toy, a back scratch or belly rub, a silly dance, or a squeal of praise.

Session Length

Keep training sessions short—but frequent! Store some treats in your pocket, and use every opportunity to turn daily events

into a mini training session. For example, ask your Frenchie to sit before giving him his food dish, or ask him to stay before following you through a doorway. Learning happens constantly, not just during set training times, so keep looking for those "teachable moments." And be consistent. If you don't want him on the couch, that mean all the time, unless you invite him up.

The Five Basic Commands

There are five basic commands you'll want your Frenchie to understand to fulfill his role as the ultimate companion dog. If you prefer training with a clicker, simply substitute a click wherever praise is indicated in the instructions that follow. Initially, reward any effort that's a step in the right direction; later, up the ante and reward only for a good performance.

Sit

This is an easy one—every Frenchie loves to sit for a treat! (You'll notice that many have an unusual sitting style, with one or both of their back legs sticking out.)

1. Standing in front of Pierre, show him a tempting treat. (Standing can be intimidating, so you may need to kneel.)
2. Move the treat close to his nose, then slowly raise it above his head, but still in front of him.

This should automatically cause Pierre to sit. Mission achieved!

3. Say "Yes! when he sits, give the reward, and praise him.

Some eager Frenchies will try jumping up to nab the treat. Reposition Pierre in a corner and kneel down so that he can't jump. Try again!

4. Once Pierre understands the concept, add a name to the command. Say "Pierre, sit!" while moving the treat.

5. Continue for several sessions, then try just saying "Sit" without using the treat. You may want to make an upward motion with your hand as you say "Sit," which gives Pierre a new visual cue to connect with.

As Pierre progresses, don't reward him every time. In Skinnerian psychology, this is called "intermittent reinforcement," and it is the most powerful way to reward. Soon Pierre will sit without a treat, on your command or hand signal. You may start leaving out the treat, but never forget to praise him each time.

Come

The key to having Pierre come when called is having something pleasant happen once he gets to you. Never ask your Frenchie to come, then scold him once he's there for something else. Would you come running to get yelled at? When

The *sit* command is easy for dogs to learn.

you need to tell him he's doing something wrong, *you* go to *him*.

1. Start by making it a game. Get down on the floor, hold out your arms, and say "Pierre, come!" in your most excited voice.

2. Say "Yes!" as soon as he starts moving toward you.

3. Give him a treat and praise after he comes to you.

At first, don't be too far away from Pierre. As he understands the "game," you can increase the distance and ask him to come when you're out of sight, perhaps in another room. And if Pierre doesn't come? That means that you're going too fast. Get closer and remember to say "Yes!" as soon as he starts to move. If he still doesn't come, go closer still and reward even a step. Once he understands what you want but chooses to ignore you, don't let him get away with not coming. Go to him and repeat the command without scolding. Just start over, which lets him know that

Use a reward to lure your Frenchie into a *down* position.

you really do expect him to come every time.

Down

I've noticed that many Frenchies don't like to learn the *down* command. Don't force the issue by trying to push him down. Bribe him! Once he knows that he'll get a reward, he won't find the idea so distasteful. This was the toughest command to teach my Simone. Now it's her favorite trick!

1. Start by asking Pierre to sit.
2. Hold that irresistible treat in front of his nose. Say "Pierre, d-o-w-n," stretching out the word as you s-l-o-w-l-y move the treat straight toward the floor. If you move too quickly, he won't have a chance to follow it and slide his front legs into a *down*.
3. If you're lucky, Pierre will follow the treat down with his head, and his whole body will go down as well.
4. Say "Yes!", treat, and heap on the praise.

When Pierre understands the command, start intermittent reinforcement and start giving the command from a standing position.

Stay

The *stay* command can be given when Pierre is in the *sit* or *down* position. It's more comfortable for him to lie down than to sit, so when you need a long *stay*, put him in a *down* command first. It's easier to teach, so we'll start with a *down-stay*.

Down-Stay

1. Give Pierre the *down* command.
2. Once he's down, give him a treat every few seconds while saying "Good *down*!"
3. After a minute or so, give him a release command (a word or phrase like "Okay!", "Free!", or "All done!) in a very excited voice to let him know that he can move again.
4. Treat again and praise him.

Once Pierre makes the connection that he's getting those treats for staying in the *down* position, you can stretch out the interval between rewards. You can also start taking a step or two away from him, increasing your distance from him. Keep at it, and soon Pierre should stay down for several minutes with you at some distance from him, only receiving his reward at the end of the exercise.

Sit-Stay

1. Standing beside Pierre, give him the *sit* or *down* command. (Don't forget to praise him!)
2. Now put your hand in front of his face and tell him "Stay."

A well-trained dog is a pleasure to live with.

3. Step away from Pierre with your right foot first, and move in front of him. Say "Good stay" in a calm voice as he stays. Hold for just a few seconds. (If he starts to move, say "Oops!" and reposition him.)
4. Step back to his side and then give a release command (a word like "Okay!" "Free!", or "All done!") in a very excited voice to let him know that he can move again.

5. Treat him and praise, praise, praise.

Work on increasing the duration of his *stay*, standing in front of Pierre longer before moving back to his side. When he gets the *stay* idea, start moving farther away from him, taking several steps. Once Pierre understands how to stay, add what trainers call "distractions." Try jumping up and down, pacing, whatever, to see if he still stays. If he "breaks" or moves out of the *stay* position, go back to Pierre, calmly reposition him, repeat "Stay," and try again.

Heel (Walk Nicely on Leash)

Most of us don't want an absolutely accurate *heel* position, as required for competitive obedience. We're happy if our Frenchie isn't pulling, and it's a bonus if he's at our side. Here's how to train for both.

Heel

1. Start in an area with few distractions. If outside, be sure that it's enclosed.
2. You can start teaching Pierre to heel with him off leash. Position him at your side. Either side will do, although heeling in formal obedience is always done on the left.
3. Show Pierre his "paycheck"—the treat. Say "Pierre, heel" and start

walking, still holding the treat at your side.
4. Give him a treat every few steps and continue.
5. When he understands that he's being rewarded for staying at your side, give fewer treats. Eventually, he will walk along at your side, waiting for a treat until you stop.

Tip: It helps to walk at a smart pace, which is more natural for your Frenchie's gait. Moving too slowly will confuse him, and he may sit. If he gets distracted while heeling, redirect his attention to you by waving the treat in front of him and talking to him.

Walk Nicely on Lead

1. With Pierre on a leash, begin walking with him at your side.
2. If (*when* for most Frenchies!) Pierre starts to pull on the leash, ignoring you, turn quickly and walk in the other direction.
3. He will be surprised and notice that you're going the other way, and he'll come back to your side.
4. As he rejoins you, give him a treat and tell him "Good Pierre!"
5. Keep walking and keep reversing directions every time he pulls. Eventually, Pierre will decide that he'd better pay attention to the crazy human who keeps doing

an about-face when he least expects it.

Tip: Work at keeping the leash slack. Every time it gets tight, it's time to tell Pierre he's not the leader by reversing direction. You're the one leading the walk, not him.

Finding a Trainer

Finding a skilled, professional dog trainer can be as difficult as teaching a Frenchie the *down* command. How do you tell who's good from a long list on the Internet or in the Yellow Pages? A good place to start narrowing your search is by asking your breeder, as well as other knowledgeable dog owners, for referrals. Most will be very upfront about who's good and who to avoid based on firsthand experiences. Asking a vet for a recommendation might be helpful, but unless you're sure that the vet is truly familiar with a trainer's skills and class methods, her opinion isn't really worth much more than your neighbor's. (Also, some trainers pay fees to vets for referring students, so beware of that potential bias.) Members of local dog clubs can often recommend good trainers, especially those who are actively involved in performance events.

Once you have your short list, call potential trainers to ask about their credentials, experience, training techniques, and class sizes. Also, inquire

Inquire whether you can watch a training class before enrolling, and ask for references from past clients.

whether you can watch a class before enrolling and for references from past clients. (A no to either counts as a red flag.) A prospective trainer should in turn ask about your training goals and your dog to determine whether a class is right for you. While checking out a class, look for signs of positive training and that both canine and humans students are enjoying themselves while learning. Having made your best choice, don't hesitate to drop out if harsh corrections or rough treatment is used in class—be it to a dog or a person!

Chapter
7

Solving Problems With Your French Bulldog

I s your French Bulldog a problem child? Welcome to every Frenchie owner's dilemma. The Frenchie is so darn cute that even when he's misbehaving, it's hard to stay mad at that funny face. However, if you continually turn a blind eye to wrongdoings when the bad boy turns on the charm, you run the risk of letting down your Frenchie by failing to show him what's acceptable behavior and what's not. This self-confident breed needs gentle but firm feedback when he crosses the line, and constantly ignoring bad behavior because he's so cute can lead to bigger problems that will make this companion dog not so nice to live with.

The key is consistency—if you set rules, be prepared to show that it's not okay to break them. Teach him good manners right from the start, and deal with small issues before they become big problems. And always consider why your Frenchie is misbehaving. Is he bored? Is he getting enough exercise? Is there new stress in your household that he's reacting to? Are you making it too difficult for him to resist temptation before he's ready for that much freedom? Your Frenchie would rather be *comme il faut*

Teach your Frenchie good manners right from the start.

(well behaved) and enjoy your company than be in constant time-outs.

Barking

Fortunately, most French Bulldogs don't suffer from the compelling need to bark that afflicts many small and toy breeds. It's part of the Frenchie's charm—he's far too cool and confident for frantic yapping. But there are exceptions, and one's in my house, with my dog Mitsy.

The Solution

Have I mentioned that Frenchies are stubborn? I haven't solved this one, but Mitsy and I have a compromise. She'll bark, I'll tell her not to, and she'll stop. That's the best she can do, and I'm okay with that.

If your Frenchie is barking excessively, don't yell because that will just reinforce the behavior. He will think that you've joined in the barking game too! Having a consequence that seems to be unconnected to you can be effective. For example, put some pennies in a small tin. When your Frenchie barks, throw the tin to make a noise and startle him (ideally without letting him see you do it). You don't want to hit him, just make a loud sound. Hopefully, your Frenchie will learn that when he

WHEN TO SEEK PROFESSIONAL HELP

I highly recommend training classes for all new Frenchie owners, no matter how many dogs you've had before. There's nothing like attending a weekly class to motivate owners to move beyond thinking about training to really putting in the time needed. Class training won't necessarily cure all problems, though. Owners should never feel embarrassed to say that things are getting out of control and seek extra help. Often, a trainer can size up a situation with an objective outsider's perspective and recommend solutions that owners can't see for themselves. The big red flag is aggression—aggression to other dogs and humans should never be tolerated. If your Frenchie is showing signs of real aggression, not just normal rough puppy play, seek professional help ASAP!

---

barks, something unpleasant happens—a big and startling noise.

Some trainers suggest training dogs to bark on command, then teaching a *no bark* command. I've never had any success with that, but you might. It seems counterintuitive, but by teaching your Frenchie to bark on command, you gain the ability to also give a command to stop the behavior. Seize opportunities when your Frenchie does bark on his own to reward him, saying "Good bark!' or "Good speak!" and then reward him with a treat. Soon, he will associate the command with his action, and you can begin asking him to bark on command. Once he understand the meaning of "Bark!" or "Speak!" you can begin adding "No bark!" to your instructions, teaching him when to stop. Always reward him after he stops.

Above all, try to analyze why your Frenchie barks. What's his trigger? For Mitsy, it's her need to tell me about possible "intruders." She can't repress that, so she's allowed to bark but must then stop. By finding out what spurs your Frenchie to bark, you can problem solve a specific solution. (For example, I should make it impossible for Mitsy to jump up into the bay window where she can see passersby, but I won't deprive her of that favorite spot.) Be creative and keep trying!

Chewing

Those Bully jaws were made for chewing! Sometimes I've thought that my puppies were part beaver because they like to gnaw on chair and table legs so much. The problem is worse when a puppy is teething, but for some Frenchies, chewing persists into adulthood. No one likes to find their favorite Jimmy Choos chewed.

HELP YOUR PUPPY BE GOOD

Make it easy for your puppy to be good by not putting him in the path of temptation. He's young, and it will take some time before he can resist that shoe or television remote, so put them out of his reach until he's older. Work on reinforcing good habits instead of always nagging him for bad behavior, and by the time he's older, he will be able to resist the puppy urges he couldn't always control. Start training young and be guided by the golden rule: If you don't want your Frenchie to do something as an adult, don't let him get away with it as a pup. It will only get worse later on. Train early, train often—and don't forget the treats!

The Solution

A two-pronged plan of action works best. First, recognize that your Frenchie needs to chew and offer him acceptable alternatives. When you catch him chewing your baseboards, tell him "No" firmly, then offer him a chew toy. (Note: The chew toy must be one he enjoys, or he won't consider it a fair trade.) He'll soon learn what's okay to chew and what's not. Keep chew toys scattered throughout the house so that he always has an option.

Second, remove temptation wherever you can. Until he makes good chewing choices, put things away or up high. (It's a good incentive to become a neat freak, even if temporarily.) Electrical cords pose special dangers, so contain that mess of wires in tubing, or tape them to the wall until you're sure that he's not interested in them.

Some things are too big to put away, like tables and chairs. I spray on a ready-made deterrent, such as a bitter apple spray and also make my own, putting a few drops of clove oil in a spray bottle of water. Bonus: Your house will smell like baking!

Some Frenchies will also chew due to separation anxiety or boredom while you're away. Offer them stuffable rubber toys filled with food or treat-dispensing toys as options. Finally, until you can be sure that your Frenchie (and your home) will be safe from shredding incidents, confine him to an ex-pen or crate when you're out to prevent him from swallowing the results of misguided chewing efforts.

Digging

Your backyard looks like the surface of the moon, with mini craters and potholes from your Frenchie's creative excavations. I've only had one digger, but she could dig halfway to China, as they say!

If your Frenchie digs in areas where she's not allowed, redirect her to a more appropriate spot.

The Solution

Much as for chewers, the key is recognizing the need to perform the behavior and offering an acceptable alternative. My Simone has one area of the yard where she's allowed—even encouraged!—to dig. I'm happy to give her space to let the dirt fly, as long as she respects my grass and flowerbeds. Reward digging in the right spots with praise and treats. Give a firm "No" if you catch your Frenchie outside those boundaries, then take him to the designated digging area. Of course, never leave your Frenchie unsupervised in the backyard—you'll be right there every time to correct him, and he will learn his limits.

House Soiling

House soiling can be a baffling problem. Suddenly, the Frenchie you worked so hard to housetrain (see Chapter 6) starts leaving unwelcome deposits and puddles. It may take you a while to notice, but suddenly the carpet starts to smell or your nose leads you to unpleasant discoveries behind chairs or in little-used rooms. What's going on?

The Solution

It's time to play pet detective. What's changed? Your search for clues starts with the Five W's:

1. Who? (If you have more than one Frenchie, which one or all of them?)
2. What? (Urination, defecation, or both?)
3. Where? (Same spot or all over the house?)
4. When? (While you're away or at home? How soon after eating? In the day or night?)
5. Why? (By looking at the other W's, you can figure out the most important W: Why?)

First, rule out any underlying health concerns. It's possible that your Frenchie has a bladder infection or upset stomach that's causing a change in bathroom habits. Have you changed food recently, for example? If your vet reassures you that all is well, look closely at the information you've gathered from the Five W's. What is your Frenchie trying to tell you? If accidents are happening while you're away, you may be asking too much of him. Try to shorten your absence, have a neighbor let him out, or give him the option of using newspaper or "wee-wee" pads. If your Frenchie is taking care to hide his errors, your first task is to (carefully) discover every location and clean and sanitize. Any remaining odors will encourage him to come back to the same location. You may need to rent a black light from a pet supply store to really find all traces of urine.

If your Frenchie is unneutered and reaching adolescence, he could be starting

One option if your Frenchie is house soiling because you're gone too long is to try using newspaper.

marking behaviors. You know the fix for that! A temporary solution to remind him that marking in the house is not acceptable is to have him wear a "belly band," which will make him think twice about lifting his leg. This should not be kept on at all times, however. Sometimes even dominant girls will "mark," usually by wetting your bed—not a fun thing to discover as you head for some shut-eye! This is her way of saying that she's the boss. Show her that she's not by removing her bed privileges (if she sleeps with you) and/or keeping the bedroom door shut.

Sometimes you won't be able to figure out why the house soiling is occurring. Whatever the reason, the way to stop the behavior is to go backward. Start treating your Frenchie like a puppy again, and repeat all of the stages of housetraining: Limit his space and opportunities for error; put him and yourself back on a schedule for mealtime and trips outside, and crate him at night if necessary. While you're working on retraining, keep your instincts sharp for any possible clues to explain your Frenchie's regressive behavior. Are you spending less time with him? Is there a new baby or puppy in the house? Is he getting less exercise? Keep thinking, clean up meticulously, and don't slip into punishment mode— stick to retraining those good habits.

COPROPHAGIA

Yuck—gross! My Frenchie's eating his poop! How can I make him stop?

Your Frenchie's not alone in this behavior says Dr. Fiona Kilpatrick, who's earned the title of "The Bulldog Vet" for her experience with the special health concerns of "bully" breeds, including French Bulldogs. Poop eating even has a fancy name: coprophagia. Very rarely, its cause is pica, a disorder that causes an abnormal appetite for strange items such as clay, ashes, and feces due to mineral deficiencies. Usually, though, the cause is more straightforward.

As distasteful as coprophagia is to humans, your dog's palate is less discriminating, and he could view fresh feces or dried-up morsels as a savory snack. A Frenchie may start stool eating out of curiosity or to keep his home clean when poop is left lying in yards or crates, then acquire a taste for it. If your Frenchie's diet isn't right for him, there may also be bits of undigested matter in his stool that he's tempted to "recycle." To stop this revolting (although not generally harmful) behavior, start with the obvious. Stoop and scoop to clean up immediately. Keep your eyes peeled for other dogs' droppings on walks, and prevent nibbling with a *leave it* command, rewarding him for passing poop by. Reduce long unsupervised periods so that he can't indulge his new gastronomic fetish, and find a more digestible diet if needed. Some owners try to "booby trap" stools in the yard by dosing them with cayenne or hot sauce, but this often won't deter Frenchies from "unseasoned" stools. Other options to try: over-the-counter products that make stool unpalatable and home remedies such as adding fresh pineapple or papaya to the diet.

Jumping Up

I love it when my Frenchies jump all over me, especially when I return after a "long" absence of 15 minutes or so. Others, however, do not find snorting Frenchies clambering up their legs quite so adorable—especially if wearing shorts or stockings. Jumping up can also frighten children, possibly causing screams, leading their parents to think that your "pit bull" Frenchie is mauling them. Frenchies jumping up on others is a sign of bad manners, something increasingly not tolerated in today's world, where so many are learning to fear dogs.

The Solution

At the risk of sounding like a broken record, take steps to prevent the behavior and provide an alternative. I don't

Check It Out

SOLVING PROBLEM BEHAVIORS CHECKLIST

✓ It's easier to solve a little problem now than a big one later. Take action as soon as you notice undesirable behavior.

✓ Start by reducing opportunities for error while you work on your rehabilitation plan.

✓ Emphasize the positive while fading out the negative. Be consistent and patient, gentle but firm.

✓ Always eliminate the possibility of health issues as an underlying cause of a problem behavior, and ensure that your Frenchie's not acting up due to boredom or lack of exercise. If retraining still isn't working, seek professional help.

✓ Aggression issues—to other dogs or humans—need your serious and immediate attention. Consult a specialist before dangerous escalation, and keep your Frenchie away from trigger situations while addressing the problem.

want my Frenchies to stop jumping up on me, but I don't want them to think that everyone else is fair game. So unless I know that a person shares my appreciation for bouncing Frenchies, I give my dogs the *sit* command when greeting someone.

Prevent potential problems when people come over to visit by first putting your Frenchie in a *sit-stay* or *down-stay* as they enter. If you can't count on your Frenchie staying put, put a leash and collar on him, ask him to sit, and stand on the leash close enough so that he can't jump. Practice this and hopefully he'll soon stay sitting on his own.

It's also useful to teach your Frenchie an *off* command. Because this means "get off," not "down," you need to distinguish

that with a different command. (It's also a handy command for removing Frenchies from your favorite chair.) Next time your Frenchie jumps up on you, push him away with your hands or by raising your knees, saying "Off." Don't forget to reward him with praise and/or treats for putting all four feet on the ground again. Eventually, your voice command, "Off" will be enough.

Some trainers also teach the *up* command by patting on their chests to let their Frenchies know when it is okay to jump up.

Nipping

This is one issue you definitely want to nip in the bud, pardon the small pun. A nip is one step away from an actual bite—which could be a death sentence for your Frenchie. Nipping starts innocently as playful puppy behavior, but it's important to let your

Frenchie know, even when young, that nipping is not tolerated. I find that Frenchies use their mouths a lot when playing with each other, engaging in jaw-wrestling wars and pulling at each other's flews (lower lips). A Frenchie's mother and littermates usually teach him how hard is acceptable, and although they often look like they're hurting each other, they know their limits. However, your Frenchie may try this sort of mouth play with other breeds that may not appreciate it.

The Solution

Stop nipping when your Frenchie is still a puppy. When he mouths or bites you, make a big fuss of saying "OW!" in a very loud voice. (Your reaction might be genuine; puppy teeth are sharp! If not, fake it and overreact.) If the puppy nips you again, immediately stop the play session and walk away. If the "ouch" method doesn't seem to be working, continue saying "Ow!" but next time also give your puppy a time-out session in his ex-pen.

As your Frenchie grows from a puppy to an adolescent, you may find that he starts nipping again. Like any teenager, he's testing his boundaries. Go back to the basics you taught him as a puppy. Be firm and don't let him get away with nipping, no matter how cute or playful he is.

Some excitable Frenchies begin to nip during rough play or when they're very excited meeting someone new. Be careful not to overexcite these Frenchies,

If you don't enjoy having your Frenchie jump up to greet you and others, teach him the *sit-stay* and *off* commands.

and stop the play session as soon as a nip happens. Because nipping is often associated with jumping up, be sure to work on that too.

If your Frenchie nips you while you're petting him, it could be because of an injury or sore spot. He could be in pain, and nipping is his only way of telling you it hurts. If your Frenchie nips at you when you try to take his bone away, that's a sign of resource guarding and the beginnings of dominance and/or aggression issues. See sidebar "When to Seek Professional Help."

Chapter
8

Activities With
Your French Bulldog

L ife's good. If you ever need a reminder, just watch your Frenchie, the ultimate *bon vivant*. Every day's a new adventure for him, and his *joie de vivre* is contagious. French Bulldogs are happy to get off the couch and tag along with you, no matter how mundane the occasion. A car ride to pick up dry cleaning—what fun! A walk to the post office? *Superbe*! Meeting friends for coffee? *Fantastique*!

If you've relegated your Frenchie to a role as a couch potato, you're doing this sociable breed as disservice. Of course, your Frenchie's short legs mean that he's not a marathoner, and his flat-face breathing restrictions and heat sensitivities need special consideration. But with a bit of foresight, common sense, and planning, your Frenchie can travel with you by car and air and join in many canine-related activities. Don't leave him to languish alone—take him along and have fun together.

Traveling With Your Frenchie

Think of his history: The French Bulldog sailed across the English Channel from Britain to France and from there across the ocean to America, as well as to other far-flung countries, including Russia. This cosmopolitan breed loves to travel and enjoys a change of scenery. His small size makes him portable, and his happy-go-

Never leave your heat-sensitive Frenchie alone in the car in hot or even warm temperatures.

lucky disposition means that he adapts well to changes to his whereabouts. Here's how to make his journey fun and safe.

Travel *en Voiture*—The Car Ride

Just say "Car ride?" and my Frenchies come running. Whether it's long or short, they love a drive. On long trips, they eventually settle for a snooze, although my Tia loves looking out the window so much, she fights sleep as long as she can.

SPORTS AND SAFETY

Frolicking Frenchies are notorious for ignoring their physical limitations. As long as your dog is having fun, he'll keep on going, even to the point of dangerous overheating and hyperventilation, so owners need to learn the warning signs and stop well before the point of overexertion. The French Bulldog should never be active in extreme heat, and he needs a time-out as soon as he starts to pant heavily. Choose cooler times for play, such as early morning or evenings, look for shady locations, reduce the length and intensity of your sessions, and always carry lots of water. Frenchies overheat very quickly—don't hesitate to use that water to douse him for a rapid cool off as needed. (Also see sidebar "Is It Okay to Leap a Frog Dog?" for more on staying safe while active.)

Because Frenchies will try to sit on your lap while driving—not the safest place for them or the driver—you'll need to make your dog a secure passenger. Stopping suddenly could hurl a loose Frenchie into a windshield or make him a harmful projectile for human passengers. Look for doggy seat belts or harnesses, and accustom him to wearing one on short trips first.

If you prefer driving with your French Bulldog in a crate, make sure that it's secured with a seat belt or other restraint. Also ensure that his crate has good airflow, to prevent him from overheating. In hot climates an air-conditioned vehicle is a must, and for extra comfort, some crates can be equipped with cooling fans. He'll also enjoy a comfy pad to lie on and suitable chew toys on long trips.

Some Frenchie suffer from carsickness, but even good riders do best traveling light or on empty stomachs. Avoid feeding for three hours prior to travel; water is okay and should still be offered. Positioning his crate so that your Frenchie can see outside will also help reduce motion sickness, as will riding in the front. (On the other hand, some do better not looking out windows, so experiment.) Opening the window a crack for fresh air can also help. If your Frenchie is frequently nauseous on car rides, you can also try herbal remedies such as giving ginger pills (or even gingersnap cookies) or Rescue Remedy before the trip. Or ask your vet about some newer medications on the market.

Younger Frenchies may outgrow motion sickness, but if the problem persists, you may need to take another look at your driving style (avoid rapid stops, drive

YOUR PUPPY'S LIMITATIONS

Puppies just want to have fun, but should you wait until your Frenchie's grown before signing up for formal activities? Definitely not, but you do need to recognize his puppy limitations—growing bones and a shorter attention span. He's ready to start learning basic obedience in puppy or good manners courses as soon as his puppy vaccinations are completed, but don't expect him to compete in formal obedience until he's older. Your puppy will also enjoy learning basic agility maneuvers, but because his growth plates aren't closed, hold off on jumps until after he's a year old or stick to very low heights. Don't push him too far too fast; keep training sessions short and happy for both of you.

slowly around curves) and/or investigate behavioral retraining (go back to very short car rides at low speeds, ensuring that each is a positive experience).

Remember, your Frenchie needs to stop and stretch (and relieve himself) more frequently than some humans who prefer to hit the road and power drive nonstop to their destination. Stopping every two or three hours is a good guideline, and the break's good for human drivers too.

Because you never know if or when your vehicle may break down, I always carry water in my vehicle, no matter how short the journey, along with water bowls. Collapsible bowls made of silicone or waterproof cloth take up no space at all, or just buy extra bowls to leave in the car. And because being prepared is the best defense, I also carry a doggy first-aid kit in the trunk at all times. (See Chapter 9 for what to include.)

A few things go without saying, but I'll say them anyway. Never leave your heat-sensitive Frenchie alone in the car in hot or even warm temperatures. Cracking the window does little to prevent a vehicle from quickly becoming an oven, and parking in the shade is rarely enough. Some folks carry an extra set of keys and leave the vehicle locked, with the air-conditioning running. But if your vehicle runs out of gas or the air-conditioning fails, you could return to a dead Frenchie. Why take that risk? Another common-sense reminder: Although your Frenchie may love it, it's not safe to let him hang his head out the window. And always have him wear a collar on car rides in case the unthinkable happens and he escapes.

Travel en Avion—The Plane Ride

Yes, Frenchies can fly, but whenever possible I avoid it. I've heard too many stories about French Bulldogs perishing in the cargo holds of planes or on a hot tarmac while waiting for loading. I'd rather take longer to travel by car than spend anxious hours in-flight worrying whether my Frenchie is okay.

If you have a puppy or a small-sized Frenchie, it's often possible to fly him with you in the cabin. I've done this and even managed to relax, knowing that my Frenchie is safe under my seat. Because airline regulations vary and frequently change, always contact your carrier to check regulations for maximum sizes and/or weight restrictions. For cabin travel, you'll need a soft-sided, well-ventilated carrier. Once on board, most airlines strictly forbid taking your Frenchie out of his carrier, so consider how long your trip is and how comfortable he'll be under your seat before booking your flight. You can unzip his carrying case once on board, and don't hesitate to ask the flight attendant for ice if needed. To minimize mid-air scenes caused by your Frenchie squealing to get out or overheating from stress panting, accustom him to the carrier at home, with frequent treats, well in advance of your departure date.

Airlines charge an extra fee for dogs traveling in the cabin, and it's best to book canine cabin space at the same time as your flight. Because there are limits on how many dogs are allowed in-cabin for each flight, book early, or your flight options may be limited. Direct flights offer the fewest complications. Make sure that your Frenchie is comfortable by taking water with you, but don't feed him later than three hours prior to takeoff. Give yourself lots of time to clear security; everything takes longer with a four-footed co-passenger. You may want to invest in removable wheels for his carrier case because dogs are not permitted to walk through most airport areas.

Many Frenchies, especially those who travel to shows around the country or internationally, are frequent flyers—and

Traveling with the portable Frenchie can be an enjoyable experience.

do arrive safely. If you decide to fly your Frenchie, here are the golden rules for safe travel in cargo. Select planes with heated holds; most planes without heating won't accept dogs, although some allow owners to sign a waiver at their own risk. Don't do it! Book a direct flight, preferably early morning or late evening, when the temperatures are cooler and the staff less harried. Many airlines have embargoes on dogs in cargo during peak

If flying with your Frenchie outside of the country, be sure that his rabies vaccination is up to date, and visit your vet to obtain a health certificate.

periods such as the Christmas season and during hot months; even if they don't, it's wise to avoid these times when things tend to go wrong. If your Frenchie suffers from separation anxiety or isn't used to a crate, reconsider cargo travel for these sensitive souls. The stress of being alone in the hold can cause panic, resulting in panting so heavy they can endanger themselves.

As for cabin travel, cargo arrangements must be made in advance, ideally for the same flight as yours. Airlines will ask for your Frenchie's weight and crate dimensions. Crates must be airline approved, so be sure that yours meets regulations. On travel day, give your Frenchie one last chance to potty before entering the airport, and don't feed after three hours before flight time. You can put safe toys in his crate, and some airlines allow an interior drip-type water dispenser. If not, freeze water in a dish for his crate instead of putting water in a bowl, which will spill and chill him. Mark your crate with "Live Animal" stickers, and I always feel better taping a friendly sign to it as well, saying something like: "Hi! My name is (Pierre, or whatever). I'm a French Bulldog and am extremely sensitive to heat. Don't leave me in the sun, and keep lots of space around my crate so I can breathe. Thank you!" Also include your name, contact information, and flight details.

IS IT OKAY TO LEAP A FROG DOG?

My Frenchie loves to run and jump, and I want to try agility with him. But so many warn me it causes back problems. Is agility safe for my Frenchie?

Dachshunds do it, Corgis do it—so why not healthy Frenchies? says Ann Winsor, DVM (a.k.a. "Dr. Annie"), of Inver Grove Heights Animal Hospital in Minnesota. Dr. Winsor notes that the biggest issue for Frenchies is the condition of their backs, which should be x-rayed to check for disc disease and potential weak spots before starting agility. Your Frenchie should also have good knees, straight shoulders, and reasonable breathing. Many Frenchies love agility, including Dr. Winsor's "Richard" (Rickway's Invincibull), who competed by invitation at the 2009 AKC/Eukanuba National Championship. At trials, a run only lasts 60 to 90 seconds, not too long or strenuous for a Frenchie in good condition, says Dr. Annie. Training requires common sense: no major jumping until the growth plates close, usually after a year, and jumps should be kept lower than competitive heights during practice. Start with baby steps, teaching your Frenchie how to be safe on equipment before increasing speed, and avoid jarring stops or landings.

If flying outside of the country, be sure that your Frenchie's rabies vaccination status is up to date for your destination, and visit your vet a week before flying for a health certificate. Usually, airlines won't ask for it, but if you don't have one, someone inevitably will ask for it! Lastly, take a photo of your Frenchie and his health records with you, just in case.

Pet-Friendly Lodgings

It's becoming easier to find pet-friendly accommodations as the hospitality industry increasingly recognizes that many clients don't want to leave their best friends behind. Choices are no longer limited to dreary fourth-rate motels; today, posh five-star hotels, many chain accommodations, modern motels, charming inns, and even some bed-and-breakfasts allow dogs to sign their guest registries. An Internet search for pet-friendly accommodations returns many options, including specialized websites such as www.petswelcome.com, www.petscanstay.com, and www.dogfriendly.com. Still, dogs aren't welcome everywhere, so smart travelers do their research in advance. It's also wise to book ahead because the number of pet rooms may be limited. When booking, ask about extra fees and any other restrictions.

Frenchies enjoy any social activities that involve being the center of attention.

And be forewarned: Many pet-friendly rooms are also smoking rooms, so if that's unacceptable for you, check in advance. On the other hand, some lodgings offer special services for dogs, including pet-sitting and welcome treats.

Being a good guest with your Frenchie means that future French Bulldogs will be welcome too. Always clean up after your dog both outside and inside your room. (Carry some stain remover with you for accidents, and don't groom your Frenchie in the room.) Put an old sheet over beds to protect bedcovers, and always crate your Frenchie if he's left alone in the room.

Sports and Activities

The American Kennel Club (AKC) divides all dog breeds into seven categories, with the French Bulldog in the Non-Sporting Group. That doesn't mean that your Frenchie can't be a good sport! He may not be a typical "sporting" dog who tracks or hunts, and he won't excel at herding trials or earthdog tests, but French Bulldogs can hold their own in other official performance events and even take top honors. Also, Frenchies really shine in the field of therapy work. Because their personal mission is to adore and be adored, Frenchies enjoy any social activities that involve being the center of attention, such as visiting nursing homes, acting as team mascot at school football games, and serving as canine ambassadors at educational events for the public. They all have their talents—find what suits you both and have fun.

Agility

Talk about fun! Agility tests how well a handler can direct her dog through an obstacle course that must be completed in a numbered sequence, racing for the fastest time and most accurate performance. Course designs vary, but dogs generally weave through poles, climb over an A-frame, go through tunnels, run along a raised balance beam, navigate a teeter-totter, and leap over jumps. Dogs compete off leash, responding to a handler's voice and hand and body signals. The course is completed together; without his handler's direction, a dog doesn't know how to complete the course in the correct order.

Agility challenges both dog and human competitors to think and act quickly, and there's always a new technique or trick to learn. While the initial focus is physical—teaching your Frenchie to perform correctly on each obstacle— the ultimate challenge is putting it all together in a high-speed mind game

that's always changing. Teams compete in novice, open, and excellent levels, with progressively more difficult courses, always aiming for faster times.

Some say that Frenchies shouldn't perform agility because it puts too much strain on their not-so-balanced physique. (See sidebar "Is it Okay to Leap a Frog Dog?" for a veterinarian's opinion.) I say phooey—it's fun, and as long as your Frenchie is approved for agility by your vet and you recognize his limitations, there's no reason he can't enjoy being a leap frog. In fact, Gunny, a.k.a. Bullmarket Spirit Shogun Dragon continued to compete in—and win—agility trials with his American owner, Andrea Morden-Moore, at 11 years young!

At a conformation show, a Frenchie is judged against the breed standard.

Conformation: Bully Beauty Contests

We all think that our Frenchie is the fairest of them all, and for many of us, that's all that matters. Some brave souls, however, have the courage to put their personal opinion to the test by stepping into the show ring. This sport is called conformation, and dogs are judged by how closely they "conform," or measure up, to an ideal described in each breed's standard. Often dismissed as frivolous beauty pageants, conformation is very important to the future of each breed. Its true purpose is to preserve quality in breeding programs by evaluating whether a dog has "breed type"—the essential qualities that make a French Bulldog look like a Frenchie and not some other breed. Some subjectivity is involved in determining which dogs come closest to epitomizing the ultimate for their breed, but without the scrutiny of judges trained to understand each standard, the appearance of the Frenchie (and other breeds) could change radically according to personal whims and whatever trend is the flavor of the month.

In a dog show, winners receive points based on how many dogs they defeat, and once they've accumulated the required total, a dog earns a championship title and the right to put Ch. (Champion) in front of his name. Breeders value championship titles highly, and many only breed dogs who are champions or from champion lines.

If you're up for the challenge, you'll

Check It Out

SPORTS AND ACTIVITIES CHECKLIST

✓ Because of his unique physique, owners must recognize their Frenchies' limitations when it comes to prolonged exercise and heat.

✓ Think short bursts of activity, not marathons. Take precautions, such as carrying water and having him wear a cooling coat on warm days; limit exercise on very hot days.

✓ Frenchies love to travel, although flying in cargo can be challenging for some due to heat sensitivities and breathing concerns. Whenever possible, driving is preferable.

✓ Performance events for Frenchies include the show ring (conformation), obedience, rally-o, and agility. Always have your Frenchie evaluated by your vet before starting a new activity.

✓ Frenchies excel in therapy work and are welcome participants in programs in hospitals, schools, nursing homes, day cares, and rehabilitation centers.

need an unneutered dog "with papers"—in other words, registered with an accredited kennel club such as the AKC. Handling classes are often offered by local all-breed dog clubs and sometimes by dog trainers. Training for the show ring includes teaching your Frenchie to walk around the ring with the right gait, to "stack," or stand in a pose that shows off his features correctly, and to stand on a table for examination by a judge. It all looks easy when you see professional handlers and experienced owners do it, but it takes some practice!

If you get bitten by the show bug, you'll find yourself driving for hours to attend shows in your area or cheerfully paying for overnight accommodations to pursue a purple ribbon or rosette that costs less than a dollar. If you lose, you won't be the only one, and you can comfort yourself by knowing that you'll still be taking your favorite dog home, regardless of what the judge thinks. Warning: Winning is a real adrenaline rush and can be highly addictive!

Obedience Trials

Got a smart Frenchie? Or even better, one of those rare Frenchies who likes to follow orders? Then obedience may be his forte. At AKC obedience trials, you and your Frenchie work together as a team, performing a series of exercises under the instruction of a judge. All competitors

Your Frenchie will enjoy spending time with you in whatever activity you decide to participate in together.

start with a perfect score, with points deducted for each error by the dog or the handler. (Yes, you're being tested too!) A team must receive a minimum score of 70 to qualify, and each qualifying score counts as a "leg." After achieving three legs, you and your Frenchie will receive a title certificate—and the endless admiration of other Frenchie owners.

Competing in obedience with a Frenchie takes patience, persistence, a good sense of humor, and a willingness to occasionally look like a fool when he decides to play to the crowds and ham it up in the ring. Because accuracy and precision count, as well as prompt responses to commands, minor flaws such as crooked *sits* or lagging heelwork are penalized, even if your Frenchie performs the exercise correctly. Also, handlers aren't allowed to praise, treat, or talk to the dogs during exercises, making it difficult to keep some Frenchies motivated. Many Frenchie folk don't have the patience to aim for perfection with a breed that's harder to train than other, more "biddable," breeds. Still, you don't have to be a drill sergeant to get a good performance from your Frenchie, and the bond you'll develop through your team effort is deeply satisfying. For inspiration, look to the top obedience Frenchie team of all time as your role models: American Hope Sylvain and "Joy," a.k.a. OTCH Marianette Joyeuse Cuvée Sylvain UDX CGC, who achieved five High in Trial (HIT) awards, as well as a perfect score of 200 in Utility. It isn't easy—but it can be done!

Rally Obedience

For those who think that competitive obedience is too stiff and serious but find that agility is too fast and athletic, there's a new performance event that combines the best of both—rally obedience, also known as rally-o or rally. Now recognized by the AKC, rally was originally devised by accomplished American obedience competitor Charles L. "Bud" Kramer, who thought that dogs and their handlers deserved to have more fun at obedience trials.

Unlike regular obedience, a dog and his handler compete without instructions from a judge, navigating their way around a numbered course, much as for an agility run but with the dog in the *heel* position. The course consists of a series of numbered stations, usually marked by pylon cones, where a sign marked with symbols indicates what exercise the team must do before going on to the next station.

Rally-o is perfect for Frenchies because owners are allowed—even encouraged!—to talk to and praise their dogs while completing the course, unlike in traditional obedience. Rally-o also allows competitors to give commands more than once if their dogs don't perform at first, another huge no-no in the obedience ring. A team should look like they're having fun, and no harsh commands or corrections are allowed. Every team starts with 200 points, with the observing judge deducting points for any errors.

Obedience purists say that rally-o is watered-down obedience for those who can't cut it under stricter formal obedience rules, but many rally-o competitors compete in obedience as well. It's a fun and welcome alternative—perfect for breeds like the French Bulldog, who'd rather not take life so seriously.

Therapy Work

Research continues to show the positive benefits that companion animals provide to humans, both physically and mentally. Recognizing this, many hospitals, rehabilitation centers, classrooms, children's centers, and nursing homes now have formal pet therapy programs. The French Bulldog is always a favorite visitor. Their funny faces and silly antics never fail to make others smile, and there are many heartwarming stories about a Frenchie's success in reaching the withdrawn when no one else could. To qualify, dogs must be sociable, enjoy pats from strangers, be calm and well mannered, and be comfortable around loud noises or unfamiliar sights, such as people walking with canes or in wheelchairs.

Many organizations have their own testing to screen dogs for therapy work; others also require certification from outside associations, such as the AKC's Canine Good Citizen test, as a prerequisite. Therapy Dogs International (TDI) and the Delta and Alpha Societies offer programs in many areas, as do many smaller local groups. Or start some "therapy" work on your own by taking your Frenchie to visit shut-ins or a day care.

Still More Fun For Frenchies…

Do you like dancing? Then try freestyle

Frenchies are favored therapy dogs because of their sociability and silly antics.

obedience, where your Frenchie becomes your partner in choreographed dance moves of your own design. Frenchies pop up everywhere doing the unexpected: kayaking (wearing life preservers, of course); riding in wagons behind cyclists; and a few, including "Jubilee" Libellule Beautiful Lady even compete in flyball, racing over hurdles to retrieve a ball. A good goal for every Frenchie is proving he has what it takes to be a good family and community member by passing the AKC's Canine Good Citizen test. Dogs are tested in ten exercises, which simulate real-life situations such as behavior in crowds, basic manners, and interaction with other dogs.

Health of Your
French Bulldog

W hen the French raise a glass to offer a toast, they say *"A votre santé!"* or simply *"Santé*!" (translation: "To your health!"). A healthy Frenchie is definitely a goal worth celebrating. Aside from any genetic conditions that nature may have dealt your French Bulldog, the biggest influence on his health is you, his owner and advocate. You don't have to immerse yourself in medical training to ensure his well-being, but knowing the basics goes a long way toward keeping him hale and hearty

Your Frenchie's Vet

Finding the right vet for your French Bulldog is extremely important. Vets are like doctors; most are competent but some really shine. Of course, the latter is the kind of vet you want for your Frenchie, and ideally you'll also find a vet who's experienced in the special health concerns of Frenchies, Bulldogs, or other flat-faced breeds. Finding a vet who's right for you as well as your Frenchie takes time, so don't wait for an emergency—start your search now!

Where to Start

A great place to start is by asking other Frenchie owners which vet they use and why. A passionate recommendation from someone with firsthand experience is much more helpful than a random search of ads in Yellow Pages listings or other directories. Don't know other Frenchie fanatics? Seek them out at local meet-up groups or dog parks, or contact a local all-breed club for other Frenchie owners or breeders in your area. Your own breeder may also be a good resource.

Searching online is another option. Ask for advice on various French Bulldog chat lists, or send an e-mail to a regional or national French Bulldog club. Still not getting anywhere? Then try the veterinary medical association for your state or province. Most have online directories, as does the American Veterinary Association at www.avma.org. Another helpful resource is Carol Gravestock's French Bulldog Z website, www.frenchbulldogz. org and its database of Frenchie-friendly vets recommended by owners.

Hopefully, this research will produce a number of recommendations to look into. Now start narrowing the field with your own selection process. Check clinics' websites to see how well they'd work for you. Are locations and business

Because of his unique health issues, finding the right vet for your Frenchie is extremely important.

hours convenient? Is parking available? Does the description of the clinic include emergency services or any specialized expertise or equipment your Frenchie might need?

Test the Waters

Now that you have a shorter list of good prospects, it's time to test the waters with some preliminary phone calls or a pre-screening onsite visit. When calling, be upfront that you're looking for a new vet who's knowledgeable about bully breeds. If cost is an issue for you, ask about prices but be sure to compare apples to apples because clinics include different services in their rate. (And remember, price isn't everything—the cheapest clinic won't necessarily be the best.) If there are multiple vets at the clinic, ask who decides which you'll see. (Some owners prefer one regular vet; others are comfortable with a team approach. Either can work, but make sure what's offered

NEW RESEARCH ON SPAYING AND NEUTERING

Spay or neuter your Frenchie to avoid unwanted pregnancies, of course. But don't be in a rush. Those reproductive organs you find so inconvenient in your Frenchie actually have an important job to do in providing hormones during his growth to adulthood. New research published in the *Journal of the American Veterinary Medical Association* shows reasons to challenge the knee-jerk advice to neuter early, neuter always, for health benefits. Although there are benefits to spaying and neutering, such as reduced incidences of some cancers and reproductive illnesses, other health problems may also occur.

In male dogs, problems after castration can actually outweigh benefits, except when aggression is an issue. For females, the topic is more complicated because unspayed females do have a higher risk of breast cancer, as well as life-threatening pyometra (infected uterus), so spaying is still recommended. On the whole, most pet owners will decide to spay or neuter their Frenchies, but be aware that neutering before three months is no longer recommended. The latest advice is to spay females after six months but before their first season (to reduce breast cancer risks) is most beneficial. Neutering of males should be done once the dog is fully grown if deemed necessary for behavioral reasons. Overall, the latest research still shows more pros than cons about neutering but presents a strong case against legislated mandatory neutering of dogs at ages as early as four months, currently proposed by some states.

works for you.) If you like the responses, ask about scheduling an introductory meeting and tour of the clinic. (Often there's no fee for this initial visit.) If the receptionist is rude or unhelpful, you may want to cross that clinic off your list right then. Or if you have time, skip the phone call and drop by the clinic for a firsthand impression. Is it clean and orderly, with friendly staff? If what you see checks out, ask the receptionist about a new-client visit with a Frenchie-friendly vet.

Take your Frenchie with you on this intro meeting, and note his response to the vet. And check your reactions as well. Because you will be interacting with the vet on your Frenchie's behalf, your goal is to find a vet you "click" with enough to establish long-term rapport. Take a list of written questions and do your own mini interview about the vet's qualifications, including Frenchie experience and what the clinic offers. Be prepared to go through this process at several clinics if necessary. Give ratings, review your notes, and then book a real appointment for a general health checkup with your best prospect, where you can further evaluate the vet in action. If you're not happy at that appointment, keep your ears open and keep searching.

Annual Vet Visits

You know how important annual checkups are for your own health, and it's the same for your French Bulldog. Dogs also age faster than we do, meaning a lot can change in their health in a year's time. Even if your Frenchie doesn't have current health issues, always make a wellness exam part of his yearly schedule. A thorough annual examination gives your vet an overall picture of your Frenchie's health. Comparing this to results from the previous year, your vet can recommend how to keep your Frenchie in tip-top condition or put him on a healthier path. Another important benefit of seeing a vet annually is early detection of small problems long before these turn into serious symptoms.

At a wellness exam, your vet will check all of your Frenchie's vital signs, including temperature, pulse, breathing rate, and body weight, as well as his heart, lungs, eyes, ears, teeth, and mouth. In fact, your Frenchie will be examined head to toe as your vet checks for anything out of the ordinary, such as lumps, bumps, or rashes, and palpitates his internal organs.

Depending on this exam, your vet may also suggest further tests, such as X-rays, fecal and urine tests, or blood work as needed. Blood tests are invaluable to check the conditions of internal organs, such as liver and kidneys, and once my Frenchies turn five I have blood and thyroid tests done annually. When your Frenchie becomes a senior, it's wise to increase your wellness visits (and possibly blood tests) to twice a year.

Make the most of these annual visits by preparing a list of questions in advance, as well as any information on recent changes in your Frenchie's health or behavior you'd like to discuss. You worked hard to find that great vet; now reap the rewards by using the annual visit as an ideal opportunity to pick her brain to learn more about the best care for your Frenchie.

Annual checkups are essential for your Frenchie's health.

Vaccinations

If you're looking for an easy answer on what vaccinations your Frenchie needs and how often, those days are gone. The new reality is that every dog is different, and a variety of factors should be considered in deciding what's right for your particular Frenchie. Vaccinations aren't "one size fits all," and vets who use the same vaccination protocol for every dog haven't been doing their homework to keep up with the latest medical findings.

Research now shows that the immunity periods given by vaccines last much longer than previously thought and that overvaccinating can be as harmful as undervaccinating. Most humans don't need annual booster shots to maintain immunity against diseases, and various university studies now show that's the case for most dogs too. Also, just because a vaccination exists for a disease doesn't mean that your Frenchie necessarily needs it. Vaccinations should be given based on his individual risk factors, including how prevalent a particular disease is in your area, how often his lifestyle might expose him to that disease, and his overall health and age.

You'll find two hardcore schools of thought on vaccinations: those who adamantly insist on vaccinating annually for every disease and those who just as passionately swear all vaccines are harmful. Making an informed choice without hours of research is difficult, but a helpful starting point is the recommendations of Dr. Jean Dodds, a researcher and veterinarian who's devoted years to the study of immunization.

Core and Noncore Vaccines

Dr. Dodds recommends different protocols depending on whether a vaccination falls into the core or noncore category. (To further your education on this evolving topic, review Dr. Dodds' website at www.itsfortheanimals.com, as well as the schedule suggested by the American Animal Hospital Association [AAHA] at www.aahanet.org, last revised in 2006.)

A variety of factors should be considered in deciding which vaccinations are right for your particular Frenchie.

Core

Dr. Dodds classifies distemper, parvovirus, and rabies shots as core vaccinations that all puppies should receive, with annual boosters at one year of age. After one year, she recommends testing immunity levels for distemper and parvovirus every three years with titer blood tests and revaccinating only if needed. Rabies boosters are still required by law, generally every three years in most states.

- **Distemper:** A viral, highly contagious, and potentially fatal disease that most often affects puppies, although adults aren't immune. Initial symptoms include watery eyes, a runny nose, sore throat, and a raised temperature, progressing to diarrhea and convulsions. Treatment includes constant nursing care, but prevention through vaccination is the best solution.

- **Parvovirus:** Another serious, potentially life-threatening viral disease, most prevalent in puppies. This very contagious virus attacks the intestinal tract, causing further complications and infection. Early signs include lethargy, vomiting, and loss of appetite, followed by very foul and often bloody diarrhea. Treatment must be rapid and intensive, with antibiotics,

IV fluids, and often plasma transfusions. Vaccinating puppies is the best prevention.

- **Rabies:** Although incidents are rare, rabies is nearly always fatal. Prevention is taken very seriously, with immunization mandated by law because rabies is "zoonotic," or transmissible to humans. Early symptoms vary but lead to full-blown aggression and tell-tale foaming at the mouth.

Noncore

Noncore vaccinations include bordetella, coronavirus, giardia, leptospirosis, and Lyme disease. Research now shows that these vaccinations are often ineffective against the many virus strains for each disease, and/or their side effects are worse than the disease itself. If you live in an area with a high risk of Lyme disease, the vaccine may be advisable, but for most states it's unnecessary. If your vet recommends noncore vaccinations, ask why they're necessary and for the supporting research before making your decision.

- **Bordetella:** A highly contagious respiratory disease also known as "kennel cough," generally caused by the parainfluenza virus. The usual symptom is a dry hacking cough, sometimes followed by retching. Mild cases often resolve on their own; more severe cases are treated with antibiotics and cough suppressants.
- **Coronavirus:** Another highly contagious viral infection, rapidly affecting the intestinal tract, causing nausea, vomiting, and diarrhea. Severity ranges from no symptoms to severe illness. This disease is rarely fatal and is treated with supportive care, which may include antibiotics and IV or injectable fluids.
- **Giardia:** A parasitic infection transmitted through contaminated water, food, or fecal matter. Gastrointestinal symptoms include vomiting and diarrhea. Treatment is usually with medication.
- **Leptospirosis:** A bacterial disease often transmitted

ANESTHESIA ANXIETY

I've heard that French Bulldogs have special anesthesia concerns. What do I need to know to make sure that my Frenchie's safe in surgery?

Because of the French Bulldog's flat face and the brachycephalic syndrome complication that often goes along with it, extra caution is a must when a Frenchie undergoes surgery or is sedated. Dr. Ann Winsor of Inver Grove Heights Animal Hospital in Minnesota offers the following tips to reduce the danger:

- Have blood work done to check for hidden problems, as well as a complete physical.
- Choose a vet who's familiar with bully breeds and their appropriate anesthesia protocol. In most cases, the preferred drugs are propofol for sedation, followed by isoflurane or sevoflurane during surgery.
- Monitoring during surgery is a must. Aside from the surgeon, another skilled professional should be present to constantly check heart rate and rhythm, blood pressure, and oxygen levels.
- Generally, Frenchies should be intubated (have a tube inserted down their throat) to keep the airway unobstructed. The tube should not be removed until the Frenchie is fully alert post-surgery.
- A Frenchie should receive the extra support of IV fluids during surgery (which also allows for the quick administration of drugs if problems develop).
- As a preventive measure, Frenchies should be placed on oxygen prior to and during the recovery phase of anesthesia. They should also be placed on heated blankets or tables during surgery
- The recovery period is just as critical as the surgery. Frenchies should be closely monitored during this time.
- Sedation over and above the anesthesia used can dangerously lower blood pressure and is generally not recommended. Ideally, "ace" (acetylpromazine) should not be used.

Most importantly, don't be shy. Grill your vet about anesthesia protocols. What drugs will she use? Will your Frenchie be monitored during and after surgery? What emergency measures are in place if things go wrong? Use the points above as a checklist to ensure that all precautions will be taken. Your Frenchie is depending on you.

through contaminated water, soil, or contact with urine from carriers, including rodents, raccoons, and other dogs. Lepto affects the liver or kidneys or both simultaneously. Affected dogs experience vomiting, fever, lethargy, excessive thirst, and jaundice. Antibiotics are the treatment of choice.

- **Lyme disease:** A tick-borne disease that is passed into the bloodstream if *affected* ticks remain on your dog for more than 48 hours. Diagnosis is difficult because Lyme presents in a variety of ways, from no obvious signs of infection to fever and a crippling arthritic syndrome. Early treatment is with antibiotics; if delayed, Lyme can become a chronic condition.

Breed-Specific Health Concerns

Warning! Contents of this section may alarm some readers. All joking aside, the list of health conditions that French Bulldogs are prone to can seem overwhelming. I was reminded of this when a prospective Frenchie owner recently contacted me for advice after researching the breed. Aren't any of them healthy? she asked with concern.

Yes, many Frenchies are healthy, but problems do exist, just as in any breed. More than 300 genetic hereditary defects have been documented in dogs, including mixed breeds. French Bulldogs fall about mid-range for health issues, with fewer defects than some breeds and more than others. Conscientious breeders do their best to minimize the occurrence and severity of problems by using dogs in their breeding programs who have passed health testing. Still, even two healthy parents can produce less than perfect puppies when the genetic dice takes an unexpected tumble.

The reality is that some health problems are built into the French Bulldog because of the breed's conformation; it is defined in canine terminology as a brachycephalic (flat-faced, short-muzzled), chondrodysplastic (dwarf) breed. The Frenchie look we find so appealing—his flat face, stubby body, stumpy tail, and short legs—increases his susceptibility to certain breathing and spinal conditions. There's no need to panic, though! Although his body structure won't win marathons or stand up to days hunting in the field, a healthy Frenchie can have a happy and active life as long as these common breed traits aren't overly exaggerated.

Brachycephalic Syndrome

It sounds like some kind of dinosaur, but "brachycephalic" is just a fancy term for dogs with pushed-in faces, like Pugs, Shih Tzu, Boston Terriers, and of course, the French Bulldog. The word comes from Greek roots: "brachy" meaning short and "cephalic" meaning head.

Changing anatomy to create a flat-faced look has resulted in other changes that can affect different areas of the respiratory tract. When breathing problems result, the overall umbrella of conditions is referred to as brachycephalic syndrome. Fortunately, most Frenchies don't have problems in every possible area of the syndrome and only show mild symptoms, such as snoring or snuffling when excited. When severe, however, brachycephalic syndrome may require surgery for a Frenchie's comfort and health. Here are some problems that can be part of brachycephalic syndrome:

Breathing Issues

For many Frenchies, breathing issues that result from their brachycephalic formation are mild—until extra stress is added. That could be the added strain of breathing hard on a hot day, a prolonged play period, or even simple excitement. This sets a vicious circle in motion that can quickly turn dangerous if it continues. As the dog tries harder to breathe, the throat begins to swell, which further blocks airways, making breathing even more difficult. The harder the Frenchie pants, the worse things get. This is why Frenchies are so susceptible to heatstroke. Learn the earning warning signs, recognizing when your Frenchie's breathing turns from normal snuffles to raspy wheezing—and act fast to cool and calm your Frenchie. Better yet, be proactive about preventing a life-threatening situation by keeping your Frenchie cool and stepping in before he's close to his limit for exercise or excitement.

Elongated Soft Palate

The Frenchie's face is shortened, but often the soft tissues of his mouth and throat aren't. Because everything doesn't fit into the smaller space, the soft palate, a mobile flap separating the nasal passages from the oral cavity, tends to hang down loosely into the throat and obstruct the airway. The result is those typical snorty Frenchie sounds, which become more pronounced during exercise or when a Frenchie is overexcited or overheated. Most Frenchies have a somewhat elongated soft palate, but when it's too long, the result is chronic airway obstruction (CAO). Typical symptoms include gagging, regurgitating frothy foam when excited or after mild activity, and lots of heavy mouth breathing. Usually, anesthesia is required to properly assess the condition, and if severe, surgery to shorten the soft palate is generally done at the same time.

Because of their pushed-in faces, French Bulldogs are prone to breathing problems.

Reverse Sneezing

It's not a disease and doesn't really bother Frenchies. But because reverse sneezing can be very scary to owners when it first happens, it's worth explaining. Sometimes Frenchies will suddenly make extra-strange noises, a honking and gasping like they're strangling or having a seizure. It sounds like they're suffocating, but it's actually the "mechanosensitive aspiration reflex," more descriptively called reverse sneezing. Instead of sneezing air out, your Frenchie rapidly sucks air in. You watch in horror as it looks like he is dying, but then it's over and he goes back to whatever he was doing with no after-effects. The exact cause isn't known, but brachycephalic breeds seem to do this backward sneeze more

often than other breeds. It's usually over quickly, in seconds to less than a minute. If you want to help stop an episode, cover your Frenchie's nose. This will force him to open his mouth to breathe, and inhaling will usually resolve the honking. You could also lightly massage his throat. If reverse sneezing happens several times a day, have your Frenchie checked by a vet for more serious problems.

Stenotic Nares

In nontechnical language, this means narrowed nostrils. When a dog inhales, the nostrils collapse on themselves, restricting air intake. Surgical correction can be done to enlarge the nostrils in extreme cases.

Hip Dysplasia

Hip dysplasia is a condition in which the head of the thighbone (femur) doesn't fit properly into the hip socket. Many Frenchies have mild hip dysplasia, which seems to bother them less than other breeds with comparable degrees of displacement. (Vets are often left shaking their heads after looking at Frenchie hip or spine X-rays, wondering how the bones can look like that without a dog showing symptoms of pain or limping.) On the other end of the spectrum, hip dysplasia can be crippling and require surgical correction, or it could require ongoing supportive care with pain and anti-

To help relieve some of the symptoms of hip dysplasia in your Frenchie, keep him at a healthy weight.

inflammatory medications. One or both hips can be affected, and often symptoms don't show up until later years, when the condition is further worsened by arthritis caused by abnormal wear on hip joints. Obesity worsens the condition, while keeping a Frenchie in good muscle tone, at a lean weight, helps lessen symptoms. Some Frenchies also suffer from elbow dysplasia in their front legs as well.

Patellar Luxation
Patellae are a dog's kneecaps; luxation means that they slip out of place. Patellar luxation ranges from very mild (the dog occasionally bunny hops, holding a back leg in the air for a few steps while the kneecap self-corrects, sliding back into place) to severe (a permanent and painful dislocation when the leg can no longer support a dog's weight). Often patellar luxation occurs in one rear leg only. Moderate cases often cause aggravation that results in arthritis in later years; severe cases may require surgery.

Spinal Conditions
In addition to being brachycephalic,

FIRST-AID KIT

Be prepared! The following list includes common items to keep on hand, which you can add to or subtract from depending on your Frenchie's personal needs. These are for minor short-term ailments you can deal with at home or quick fixes until you can seek emergency care only. If symptoms such as diarrhea or vomiting persist, always see a vet.

- 3% hydrogen peroxide solution (Note: Call your vet immediately and do not induce vomiting if your Frenchie isn't fully alert or if he's swallowed strong acid or base or petroleum products, such as household cleaning supplies, dishwasher detergents, or gasoline.)
- activated charcoal
- adhesive bandages
- antibiotic ointments
- antihistamine
- antiseptic creams
- aspirin
- bulb syringe: to help clear vomit and other messy secretions
- cotton balls and swabs
- cotton gauze bandage wrap
- cotton gauze pads
- disinfectants
- emergency ice packs
- eye dropper
- first-aid tape
- heating pad and/or hot water bottle
- Kaopectate
- nonsteroidal ophthalmic ointment
- Pedialyte or other balanced electrolyte fluid
- penlight
- petroleum jelly
- rectal digital thermometer (normal dog temperature range is 100.5° to 101°F (38° to 38.3°C).
- saline solution
- small scissors (one with blunt end)
- tweezers
- Vet Wrap
- zinc oxide cream

the French Bulldog is also a chondrodysplastic, or "dwarfed" breed. This is a condition in which the torso develops normally, but the long bones of the limbs are thicker and shorter than usual. Although considered a genetic deformity in most breeds, this bone structure is the norm for Frenchies, giving the breed its distinctive heavyset, "big dog in a small package" look.

Chondrodysplasia visibly affects the limbs, but impacts other bones we can't see in the body as well, including the spine. Problems more common in chondrodysplastic breeds include malformations of spinal vertebrae, or hemivertebrae, and a higher incidence of intervertebral disk degeneration (IVDD). Responsible breeders strive to preserve the desirable external look that results from chondrodysplasia while minimizing its unintended, unhealthy consequences. Before breeding, French Bulldogs should be x-rayed to assess the condition of their spines, and many breeders also x-ray their puppies' backs as a safety check before placement with owners.

If your Frenchie seems unusually lethargic, contact your veterinarian.

Hemivertebrae

The spine is made up of vertebrae, or backbones, connected by the spinal cord and cushioned by spongy disks that act as shock absorbers. Chondrodysplastic breeds are more prone to abnormally or partially formed vertebrae. These misshaped vertebrae, or hemivertebrae, are further classified into different types—block, wedge, butterfly, transitional, etc.—as well as according to their formation and where they're located in the spine. Hemivertibrae are a spinal deformity that's congenital, or present at birth, not something that develops later as the puppy grows.

Many Frenchies have hemivertebrae (or hemis), and the impact on their health can range from none at all to crippling and paralysis. Puppies can

be x-rayed as early as 10 to 12 weeks to check for hemivertebrae, but analysis is best left to orthopedic specialists or vets who've reviewed many, many spinal X-rays. There's no simple rule—one hemivertebrae in the neck area can be very serious, while as many as six over the rib-cage area may be harmless. An experienced vet considers many factors when assessing whether hemivertebrae will cause future problems: How badly deformed is each? Are there several consecutive hemis and are they fused? Which section of the spine are they in? Do they affect the overall shape of the spine?

Hemivertibrae that twist the spine can result in painful conditions known as kyphosis, scoliosis, and lordosis. Hemis can also compress the spinal cord, causing paralysis, pain, rear-limb weakness, and incontinence. Frenchies with very short backs are often more prone to hemivertebrae because the shorter back causes more compression of vertebrae, but this is just a general rule. For extreme cases, surgery may be required. On the other hand, many Frenchies with hemis will live their whole lives symptom-free. Wise owners will know the condition of their Frenchie's spine, hopefully from x-rays done before purchase, and take precautions if required. For example, French Bulldogs with spinal problems shouldn't jump off couches.

Intervertebral Disk Degeneration (IVDD)

Intervertebral disk degeneration (IVDD) is a disease that generally occurs between four and seven years of age. Degeneration of the disks between the bony vertebrae of the spine causes them to change from a rubbery cushion to a rigid material, which can then escape from between vertebrae and push into the spinal cord. Result: a "slipped," or herniated, disk that can paralyze an apparently healthy Frenchie in days. This often happens after a sudden jump or fall.

Signs to watch for include a Frenchie who yelps suddenly when touched or picked up,

a stiff or wobbly gait, dragging of the rear feet, or an arched back. Prompt treatment is critical. Drugs to reduce the swelling, followed by very strict rest, will sometimes reverse the symptoms. Severe cases require surgery, which will relieve pain, although restoration of mobility can't be guaranteed. Some Frenchies remain paralyzed but function well in special carts post-surgery.

General Health Concerns

Don't be alarmed by the health conditions described in this section—not every Frenchie will experience these problems. Every breed is prone to certain conditions, and Frenchies don't have some of those more common in other breeds. For example, heart conditions are rare, and cancer isn't as prevalent. Unspayed females are prone to mammary tumors, as is true for all breeds, and the incidence of mast cell cancer in French Bulldogs is slightly higher than for other breeds. But generally, cancer strikes older Frenchies only. Epilepsy isn't common, and incidence rates for other health concerns, like kidney disease, diabetes, and deafness are no higher than general canine averages. Although good health can't be guaranteed, choosing a Frenchie from health-tested parents screened for the breed's most common problems is the best defense.

Allergies

Oh, that itch! Allergies can be as frustrating for owners as for their dogs, as they constantly search for new ways to ease the constant scratching, foot chewing, licking, rubbing, and other forms of self-mutilation. The root cause is an overactive immune system that attacks itself, but until relief is found, owners often feel helpless as various remedies fail and the situation worsens. And things can worsen a great deal. Minor itchiness or small bumps can turn into an endless cycle of secondary skin infections, such as seborrhea, hair loss, alligator-like skin, and even wounds from constant licking (lick granuloma) if not attended to.

Any breed can have skin allergies, and the French Bulldog is no exception, although some lines seem more prone than others. Frenchies are generally more prone to food sensitivities than full-blown allergies. Often allergies are environmental (grasses, pollens, molds, house dust, mites, laundry detergents, and so on), and Frenchies may inhale or come into contact with these allergens. Inhalant allergies often worsen in the spring and fall. But if a Frenchie is allergic to one thing, he's generally allergic to more than one, and diet should always be investigated.

Some dogs are allergic to environmental things, such as grasses and pollens.

Sorting out the offending substances is the big challenge. Once identified, an owner can seek to eliminate or reduce his Frenchie's exposure. A multipronged attack usually works best: Start strengthening the immune system and providing relief from the itch while figuring out what the underlying allergen(s) are. For treatment, a combination of alternative and conventional medicine works well, and owners should investigate both approaches. Consulting a vet with training in alternative therapies or a skin specialist is extremely helpful; otherwise, owners may invest considerable time and energy in a trial-and-error process while their Frenchie's condition continues to deteriorate.

In the worst cases, a Frenchie may need lifelong allergy serum injections and ongoing drug treatment. Other alternatives that often provide good results include bathing with a special medicated shampoo, changing your Frenchie's diet, and keeping the house extra clean. Check with your vet on the best course of action for your individual dog.

Digestive Problems

Anyone who's experienced the infamous "Frenchie perfume" knows that this charming breed can pass some not-so-adorable gas! Finding the proper diet helps. (See sidebar "Oh, That 'Eau De Frenchie!'" in Chapter 4.) But for more extreme cases, the underlying cause could be digestive issues such as colitis or inflammatory bowel disease (IBD), which may also be accompanied by diarrhea and vomiting. Special diets and medication can control these diseases, which are generally chronic.

Parasites

Parasites are highly unpleasant organisms that survive by drawing nourishment from their "host," which could be your unsuspecting Frenchie. Some canine parasites then move on to take residence in you. Depending on the parasite type and the degree of infestation, these pests cause problems ranging from mild or no symptoms to malnutrition, anemia, diarrhea, and even death. Don't let these freeloaders stick around—prevent or treat promptly.

External Parasites

As their name suggests, external parasites live on the outside of your dog, on his hair or skin.

Fleas

Fleas are tiny, wingless but highly agile insects that live off the blood of mammals. Their bite causes itching, scratching, skin problems, and secondary infections. While uncommon in dry, cold climates, fleas are real pests in hot, humid areas. Ask your vet about various topical and oral medications aimed at killing fleas in the egg, larvae, and adult phases. But do your own research as well because some medications are overkill and can harm your Frenchie. Homeopathic remedies such as cedar oil, lavender, and rosemary may work. For best results, focus on creating a less flea-friendly home environment. Add dehumidifiers, vacuum frequently, reduce carpeting, wash bedding often, and use nontoxic products such as borax and diatomaceous earth.

Ticks

Ticks are another bloodsucker, but they are much larger than fleas. Ticks are actually an arachnid, closer to spiders than bugs. Unlike flea bites, your Frenchie may not even notice when ticks latch

HEALTH CHECKLIST

✓ The French Bulldog is generally a sturdy, healthy dog but does have some specific health concerns.

✓ These are mainly related to his structure as a brachycephalic (flat-faced), chondrodysplastic (dwarf) breed. His flat face can result in breathing issues, and Frenchies are more prone to back problems than nondwarf breeds.

✓ Other possible health concerns: skin issues caused by allergies, digestive problems, patellar luxation (slipping kneecaps), and hip dysplasia.

✓ Selecting a Frenchie from health-tested parents reduces the potential for problems.

✓ Finding a veterinarian familiar with the Frenchie's specific health needs is very important for his ongoing health. Make annual wellness visits part of your Frenchie's health schedule.

✓ Vaccinations are no longer one size fits all. Study the latest research, and consult your vet for appropriate vaccination protocol.

✓ Like any dog, Frenchies aren't immune to parasites. Learn about internal and external parasites, and remember that prevention is always preferable to treatment.

✓ Combine traditional Western veterinary medicine with alternative therapy options for a holistic approach to your Frenchie's care.

✓ Senior Frenchies have special needs, with common aging changes including decreased eyesight and hearing and possibly arthritis. Avoid obesity with moderate exercise and a high-protein, low-fat diet, and seek prompt vet advice for any health changes.

on. But because ticks can carry Lyme disease, Rocky Mountain spotted fever, and other nasty stuff, you don't want them around. In your yard, keep grass mowed and bushes trimmed, and check your Frenchie for ticks after walks in wooded or areas of tall grass. If you find a tick, put on gloves, then remove it with tweezers or a specially designed tick removal tool. Grasp as close to the skin as possible, pulling straight out without twisting and taking care to remove the tick's head. Rinse the bite area with mild soap and watch for infection. Topical tick prevention products are now available but should be used with care because they contain toxic ingredients—check with your vet. A Lyme vaccination is also now available, but its risks must be weighed against the benefits.

Ringworm

Ringworm is not a worm but a fungus that lives on the skin surface, feeding on dead skin tissues and hair. The usual symptom is a round hairless lesion or "ring." It is transmitted by direct contact with infected animals or persons and can be passed from pets to humans and vice versa. Healthy adult dogs usually have a resistance to ringworm, but puppies and those with weakened immune systems are more susceptible. Ringworm is diagnosed by skin scrapings and treated with an antifungal drug and sulphur shampoos. Contaminated environments must be cleaned with a bleach mixture to kill spores.

Internal Parasites

These troubling parasites set up camp inside your Frenchie, most commonly heading for the small intestine, although some infect the stomach, colon, heart, and other areas. Internal parasites can afflict both puppies and adult dogs, and some are transmissible to humans.

Heartworm

Spread by mosquitoes, these potentially deadly worms invade the muscles of the heart and the pulmonary artery that

Check your Frenchie for fleas and ticks after he's been playing outside.

supply blood to the lungs. Treatment involves a series of injections to kill the adult worms, but because it's very hard on a dog, prevention with heartworm medication in areas with a risk of heartworm is highly preferable. (Heartworm isn't carried by mosquitoes in cold-climate regions.) Heartworm medication is available as tablets, topicals, and injections, but because some Frenchies experience side effects, long-lasting medications (i.e., for more than one month) are best avoided.

Hookworm

Hookworms are tiny intestinal blood-sucking worms that hook onto the intestinal walls. Severe hookworm infestations can kill a puppy. They are very contagious to other pets—and transmissible to humans. Treatment is with an oral dewormer; severe cases may need plasma transfusions.

Roundworm

This is the most common internal parasite, especially prevalent in puppies. A slender, spaghetti-shaped worm, roundworm can be visible in the stool of a heavily infested dog, or its eggs will show up in fecal tests. Roundworm is treated with a deworming medication.

Whipworm

These are long, whip-shaped worms that take up residence in a dog's colon. Whipworms are treated with deworming medication.

Alternative Therapies

Treatments such as acupuncture, chiropractic therapy, herbal treatments, and homeopathy are now so common that "alternative therapies" is no longer an accurate description for their role in a Frenchie's health care. Many "conventional" veterinarians trained in Western medicine now incorporate these therapies into their range of options. Instead of thinking only alternative therapies versus only conventional medicine, it's better to seek a holistic approach—or health care that combines both, using the best of two worlds. Other treatments now offered for your Frenchie include physical rehabilitation, such as hydrotherapy, therapeutic ultrasound, cryo- and heat therapy, magnetic therapy, massage, and many more.

Western medicine tends to be "reactive," responding to problems, while alternative therapies often have a "proactive" focus, seeking to promote ongoing good health. Often, Western medicine offers short-term solutions, while alternative therapies take longer because their focus is on treating the underlying causes of an illness, not just immediate solutions. Of course, prevention is always better than a cure, so we have much to learn from alternative care.

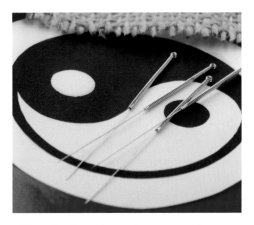

Alternative therapies, such as acupuncture, are becoming much more mainstream.

I personally use both methods for my Frenchies but would never choose one exclusively over the other. I've found that acupuncture and chiropractic therapy helped my Bulldog's arthritis, along with supplements such as glucosamine and yucca. We continue those, but now that his pain is severe, it's finally time to add the relief Metacam provides (along with milk thistle to protect his liver). I've used Chinese herbs for skin problems but will also use antibiotics if required. My best advice: Find a vet who's trained and certified in both types of medicine, or find a certified alternative therapist willing to work with your vet (and vice versa). It shouldn't be an either/or situation. Beware, however, of those who dabble in alternative therapies without proper training. And always let your vet know of any herbal supplements your Frenchie is taking because these can interact or interfere with conventional drugs. Keep learning and keep your mind open.

Senior Frenchies: *Les Vieux*

Until your Frenchie hits senior status, it's hard to understand the great joy these oldsters give. There's so much shared history and such a strong bond. Two of my bully crew are "pensioners," and I treasure every day. Sure, they don't move as fast or hear as well and their eyesight is dimming. But they have a depth and strength of character that puppies, for all their young cuteness, don't have. Living with an older Frenchie is a true reward for all the time and care you've invested to achieve the golden years.

It's the last chapter in your Frenchie's journey, and like other phases of his life, it comes with special needs. As Frenchies age, they experience the same decline that humans do, but never make the mistake of considering old age as a disease. His senses aren't as sharp and his muscle strength not as strong, but your senior Frenchie is still a vital companion who deserves your time and attention. Don't stop taking him for walks or playing with him. Exercise will be gentler, and you may need to find less vigorous games, but staying active is key to preserving his mental and physical health.

Caring for your Frenchie well when he's young will positively impact his later years.

Diet Change

Your senior will need a diet change to prevent obesity as his activity levels decline and his stomach becomes more sensitive. Decrease the fat levels of his meals but increase the amount of protein because he now needs more. You may also need to add special supplements, for example glucosamine for joints. He may need his kibble softened with water, or he may need canned food for worn-down or missing teeth.

Grooming

Pamper your Frenchie with lots of brushing, a bed with enough cushioning and support for old bones, and drops for dry eyes. He may also need more frequent nail trims because he won't wear them down as often. Check him regularly during grooming sessions for lumps and bumps, rashes, hair loss, or other changes.

Also, be extra vigilant about keeping your Frenchie's teeth clean with regular brushing and raw bones to gnaw. (Putting older Frenchies under anesthesia for teeth-cleaning can be very risky and is best avoided.) Regular dental hygiene will also ward off that potent old-dog bad breath and prevent bacteria from entering the bloodstream via his mouth, which can damage internal organs.

Age-Specific Illnesses

Frenchies are living longer than ever, and with longer life spans come age-specific issues like arthritis, increased sensitivity to heat and chills, reduced vision and hearing, and a higher susceptibility to diseases such as cancer. Sometimes we don't notice gradual changes because they happen slowly, and unseen changes may also be happening, which could be the start of serious illnesses. To stay on top of your Frenchman's health needs, increase vet visits to twice annually and do regular blood work testing, including checking thyroid levels. You may also need to add in extra services like acupuncture or water therapy to ease aching joints.

Pay attention to changes such as weight loss, poor appetite, swellings, lameness, coughing, increased thirst and drinking, and changes in muscle tone. Geriatric diseases to watch for include cataracts; Cushing's syndrome (overproduction of the adrenal hormone); Addison's disease (underproduction by the adrenal gland); bladder stones; congestive heart failure (symptoms include coughing, decreased energy, and fluid buildup); and even possibly prostate disease or diabetes. Some dogs also suffer from a form of dementia called canine cognitive dysfunction (CCD). New drugs are available that may help with this condition.

Having a senior Frenchie in your life is a gift. Make his elderly years truly golden with your special care and attention. He's given you unconditional love for years. Now's the time to do your best to return that love, although as flawed humans, we'll never come close to matching true canine devotion. *Vive les Frenchies*—long may they rule our hearts! *Je vous aime, toujours.*

Resources

Associations and Organizations

Breed Clubs

American Kennel Club (AKC)
5580 Centerview Drive
Raleigh, NC 27606
Telephone: (919) 233-9767
Fax: (919) 233-3627
E-Mail: info@akc.org
www.akc.org

Canadian Kennel Club (CKC)
200 Ronson Drive, Suite 400
Etobicoke, Ontario M9W 529
Telephone: (416) 675-5511
Fax: (416) 675-6506
E-Mail: information@ckc.ca
www.ckc.ca

Federation Cynologique Internationale (FCI)
Secretariat General de la FCI
Place Albert 1er, 13
B – 6530 Thuin
Belqique
www.fci.be

French Bull Dog Club of America (FBDCA)
www.frenchbulldogclub.org

French Bulldog Fanciers of Canada (FBFC)
www.frenchbulldogfanciers.com

The Kennel Club
1-5 Clarges Street
Picadilly, London
W1J 8AB
Telephone: 0870 606 6750
Fax: 0207 518 1058
www.the-kennel-club.org.uk

United Kennel Club (UKC)
100 E. Kilgore Road
Kalamazoo, MI 49002-5584
Telephone: (269) 343-9020
Fax: (269) 343-7037
E-Mail: pbickell@ukcdogs.com
www.ukcdogs.com

Pet Sitters

National Association of Professional Pet Sitters
15000 Commerce Parkway, Suite C
Mt. Laurel, New Jersey 08054
Telephone: (856) 439-0324
Fax: (856) 439-0525
E-Mail: napps@ahint.com
www.petsitters.org

Pet Sitters International
201 East King Street
King, NC 27021-9161
Telephone: (336) 983-9222
Fax: (336) 983-5266
E-Mail: info@petsit.com
www.petsit.com

Rescue Organizations and Animal Welfare Groups

American Humane Association (AHA)
63 Inverness Drive East
Englewood, CO 80112
Telephone: (303) 792-9900
Fax: 792-5333
www.americanhumane.org

American Society for the Prevention of Cruelty to Animals (ASPCA)
424 E. 92nd Street
New York, NY 10128-6804
Telephone: (212) 876-7700
www.aspca.org

US French Bulldog Rescue Organization
www.frenchbulldogrescue.org

Royal Society for the Prevention of Cruelty to Animals (RSPCA)
RSPCA Enquiries Service
Wilberforce Way, Southwater,
Horsham, West Sussex RH13 9RS
United Kingdom
Telephone: 0870 3335 999
Fax: 0870 7530 284
www.rspca.org.uk

Sports

International Agility Link (IAL)
Global Administrator: Steve Drinkwater
E-Mail: yunde@powerup.au
www.agilityclick.com/~ial

The World Canine Freestyle Organization, Inc.
P.O. Box 350122
Brooklyn, NY 11235
Telephone: (718) 332-8336
Fax: (718) 646-2686
E-Mail: WCFODOGS@aol.com
www.worldcaninefreestyle.org

Therapy

Delta Society
875 124th Ave, NE, Suite 101
Bellevue, WA 98005
Telephone: (425) 679-5500
Fax: (425) 679-5539
E-Mail: info@DeltaSociety.org
www.deltasociety.org

Therapy Dogs Inc.
P.O. Box 20227
Cheyenne WY 82003
Telephone: (877) 843-7364
Fax: (307) 638-2079
E-Mail: therapydogsinc@qwestoffice.net
www.therapydogs.com

Therapy Dogs International (TDI)
88 Bartley Road
Flanders, NJ 07836
Telephone: (973) 252-9800
Fax: (973) 252-7171
E-Mail: tdi@gti.net
www.tdi-dog.org

Training

Association of Pet Dog Trainers (APDT)
150 Executive Center Drive Box 35
Greenville, SC 29615
Telephone: (800) PET-DOGS
Fax: (864) 331-0767
E-Mail: information@apdt.com
www.apdt.com

International Association of Animal Behavior Consultants (IAABC)
565 Callery Road
Cranberry Township, PA 16066
E-Mail: info@iaabc.org
www.iaabc.org

National Association of Dog Obedience Instructors (NADOI)
PMB 369
729 Grapevine Hwy.
Hurst, TX 76054-2085
www.nadoi.org

Veterinary and Health Resources

AKC Canine Health Foundation
www.akcchf.org

American Animal Hospital Association (AAHA)
12575 W. Bayaud Ave.
Lakewood, CO 80228
Telephone: (303) 986-2800
Fax: (303) 986-1700
E-Mail: info@aahanet.org
www.aahanet.org/index.cfm

American College of Veterinary Internal Medicine (ACVIM)
1997 Wadsworth Blvd., Suite A
Lakewood, CO 80214-5293
Telephone: (800) 245-9081
Fax: (303) 231-0880
Email: ACVIM@ACVIM.org
www.acvim.org

American Holistic Veterinary Medical Association (AHVMA)
2218 Old Emmorton Road
Bel Air, MD 21015
Telephone: (410) 569-0795
Fax: (410) 569-2346
E-Mail: office@ahvma.org
www.ahvma.org

American Veterinary Medical Association (AVMA)
1931 North Meacham Road, Suite 100
Schaumburg, IL 60173-4360
Telephone: (847) 925-8070
Fax: (847) 925-1329
E-Mail: avmainfo@avma.org
www.avma.org

ASPCA Animal Poison Control Center
Telephone: (888) 426-4435
www.aspca.org

British Veterinary Association (BVA)
7 Mansfield Street
London
W1G 9NQ
Telephone: 0207 636 6541
Fax: 0207 908 6349
E-Mail: bvahq@bva.co.uk
www.bva.co.uk

Canine Eye Registration Foundation (CERF)
VMDB/CERF
1717 Philo Rd
P O Box 3007
Urbana, IL 61803-3007
Telephone: (217) 693-4800
Fax: (217) 693-4801
E-Mail: CERF@vmbd.org
www.vmdb.org

Orthopedic Foundation for Animals (OFA)
2300 NE Nifong Blvd
Columbus, Missouri 65201-3856
Telephone: (573) 442-0418
Fax: (573) 875-5073
Email: ofa@offa.org
www.offa.org

Publications

Books

Anderson, Teoti. *The Super Simple Guide to Housetraining.* Neptune City: TFH Publications, 2004.

Anne, Jonna, with Mary Straus. *The Healthy Dog Cookbook: 50 Nutritious and Delicious Recipes Your Dog Will Love.* UK: Ivy Press Limited, 2008.

Dainty, Suellen. *50 Games to Play With Your Dog.* UK: Ivy Press Limited, 2007.

Morgan, Diane. *Good Dogkeeping.* Neptune City: TFH Publications, 2005.

Magazines

AKC Family Dog
American Kennel Club
260 Madison Avenue
New York, NY 10016
Telephone: (800) 490-5675
E-Mail: familydog@akc.org
www.akc.org/pubs/familydog

AKC Gazette
American Kennel Club
260 Madison Avenue
New York, NY 10016
Telephone: (800) 533-7323
E-Mail: gazette@akc.org
www.akc.org/pubs/gazette

Dog & Kennel
Pet Publishing, Inc.
7-L Dundas Circle
Greensboro, NC 27407
Telephone: (336) 292-4272
Fax: (336) 292-4272
E-Mail: info@petpublishing.com
www.dogandkennel.com

Dogs Monthly
Ascot House
High Street, Ascot,
Berkshire SL5 7JG
United Kingdom
Telephone: 0870 730 8433
Fax: 0870 730 8431
E-Mail: admin@rtc-associates.freeserve.co.uk
www.corsini.co.uk/dogsmonthly

The French Bullytin
www.frenchbullytin.com

Websites

Nylabone
www.nylabone.com

TFH Publications, Inc.
www.tfh.com

Index

Note: Boldfaced numbers indicate illustrations.

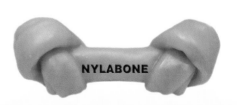

Photo Credits

Dedication

For Beau and Dixie—the two Frenchies forever in my heart who started it all.

Acknowledgments

For the three very different individuals most responsible for my French Bulldog addiction.

- Marion Anderson, Flarepath, who turned a first-time Frenchie pet owner into a breed fanatic, showing me that going to the dogs was a good thing.
- Chris Jefferies, Chrishell, for your trust in sending Mitsy all the way to Canada from New Zealand and for giving me the courage to follow my own path.
- Arlie Alford, LeBull, who taught me what a good Frenchie should look like, then helped make mine better. And whose actions constantly remind me that striving for the best is a goal worth pursuing.

And to my long-suffering husband, Derek Keeling, who indulges my Bully obsession and who pushed me to complete this project with his one constant question: "Is The Book done yet?"

About the Author

Lisa Ricciotti is an award-winning writer who lives in Edmonton, Alberta (Canada), where she writes for a variety of regional and national magazines. While Lisa is the former editor of three travel and lifestyle magazines, she now enjoys the freedom of working as a freelancer from a home base shared with three French Bulldogs and one grumpy but adorable elderly English Bulldog. Her passions are simple: chasing a good story and chasing her Frenchies. Sometimes she succeeds in combining the two, notably as managing editor for *The French Bullytin* and through projects such as this breed guide, her first book.